Urban Sociology

SOCIETY, LOCALITY AND HUMAN NATURE

PETER DICKENS
University of Sussex

HARVESTER
WHEATSHEAF

New York   London   Toronto   Sydney   Tokyo   Singapore

First published 1990 by
Harvester Wheatsheaf,
66 Wood Lane End, Hemel Hempstead,
Hertfordshire, HP2 4RG
A division of
Simon & Schuster International Group

Printed and bound in Great Britain by
Billings and Sons Ltd, Worcester

Typeset in 10/12pt Sabon
by Witwell Ltd, Southport

British Library Cataloguing in Publication Data

Dickens, Peter, 1940–
  Urban sociology: society, locality and human nature.
  1. Urban sociology
  I. Title
  307.7′6

ISBN 0-7450-0642-6
ISBN 0-7450-0643-4 pbk

---

1 2 3 4 5   94 93 92 91 90

CONTENTS

ACKNOWLEDGEMENTS

Sussex University continues to be an excellent base for interdisciplinary work and this book has benefited from discussions with students and tutors from such diverse disciplines as English, Geography, Politics, Psychology, Sociology and Urban Studies. More specifically, I wish to thank Simon Duncan, Pete Saunders and Mike Savage at the University of Keele for comments on early drafts of parts of the book. Particular thanks go to Pete: we have discussed the ideas outlined here on a number of occasions and in a number of localities.

My thanks also go to Rom Harré of Oxford University and John Urry of Lancaster University. At a late stage they made a number of extremely helpful comments.

Bill Williams, the editor of the Harvester Wheatsheaf sociology series of which this is a part, managed an excellent combination of criticism and encouragement. Clare Grist of Harvester Wheatsheaf was also very supportive.

The book was written in a converted eighteenth century bakehouse located in my garden. The most important point about this particular 'escape attempt' is that it was fully aided and abetted by my wife, Anna. Finally, I have learnt so much about human nature from my exuberant teenage daughter, Emma, that it is only right that I should dedicate the book to her.

PREFACE

This book has three closely related objectives. The first is to introduce students to the main themes of contemporary urban sociology. The second is to demonstrate how urban social theory might be extended in such a way as to recognise cities as the contexts of social interaction and the formation of personal identities. The third is to show how both the above themes relate to each other.

Chapter 1 outlines the basis for the new emphasis on human nature which is being recommended here. Drawing and elaborating on the work of Veblen, Goffman, Harré and Giddens, it shows in some detail how a new concern with human instincts and human interaction can be made systematic. It also suggests, in an introductory manner, how this work can be combined with our particular interest in localities. Fictional literature provides one way in which we can see how people's actions and priorities combine with the large-scale social processes affecting their lives.

Chapter 2 argues that the 'new' form of urban sociology suggested here is actually not all that new after all. Seventy years or so ago the Chicago School of Urban Sociology was also attempting to develop an approach which combined an emphasis on social (what they called 'cultural') processes with one which emphasised behaviour based on human instincts. These latter the Chicago School called the 'biotic' level. Since the early days of urban sociology, however, these two emphases have diverged. On the one hand, urban studies, and indeed sociology more generally, has stressed the social or 'cultural' dimension. On the other hand, psychologists and biologists have pursued the 'biotic level' of innate human drives. The chapter concludes by summarising some of the more important recent advances in the study of the 'biotic level'. It concludes, however, by arguing that these are seriously handicapped by not recognising the cultural and social relations with which biological and psychological processes combine.

The remaining chapters in the book show how the new approach outlined here (one *combining* what the Chicago School would have called the 'biotic' and 'cultural' levels) can be applied to the various fields of study represented by contemporary urban sociology. Each chapter starts by briefly reviewing the state of the art. It then demonstrates how the new perspectives outlined in Chapters 1 and 2 might be applied to the particular field of urban sociology in question. This is done by selecting a range of studies which demonstrate the broad approach being recommended here.

Chapter 3 is about employment, economic relationships and localities. The main message from contemporary urban sociology here is that localities are largely hostages to capitalist economies. People and local social systems are obliged to abide by the demands of profitability and the capacity of capital to move to localities where profits can be made. This chapter does not disagree with this analysis, but it also argues that people find ways of dealing with these overarching economic constraints and limitations. The literature outlined in Chapters 1 and 2 again helps us to appreciate the significance of work to people's identities. It is a means of sustaining personal and social esteem. To a large extent, however, esteem and personal identity are established in the realm of civil society, the sphere of social life outside work.

This brings us to Chapter 4. Again, the chapter starts by reviewing the very diverse ways in which urban sociology examines civil society. The emphasis in much of this work is on the penetration of the market into all spheres of personal and social life. But this chapter also argues that our new approach to urban sociology demonstrates how people are to a large extent able to create their own lives and 'selves' in civil society. For individuals and households (and especially those with economic, social and political power), the marketplace can be a means of realising underlying instincts; the protection of kin as well as the demand for personal identity. This is much less the case, however, for those excluded from the market. These themes are illustrated with reference to a number of themes covered by contemporary urban sociology. They include what is sometimes called 'postmodern' culture, a way of life enjoyed mainly by dominant social groups. They also include the relations formed by subcultures and contemporary home life as it is led by both middle class and subordinate social groups.

Chapter 5 is concerned with politics and the state: another major theme in contemporary urban sociology. Indeed, in the British case, the subject has acquired an especially topical significance as local and central governments continue to conflict over social and economic policies and priorities. The objective of this chapter is again to show how our new emphasis might assist in developing an improved understanding of the state. State power depends not simply on coercion. It is also a product of people's demands for security. This includes not simply material security but emotional security: one which insists on personal identity and the support of family and kin. At the same time, however, the state acts as a powerful co-ordinator and regulator of individuals' lives and relationships. The argument is that conventional sociology has great difficulty in understanding the growing tide of demands for regional or national autonomy with religious, ethnic and racial bases. The new approach outlined here helps to remedy this situation.

Chapter 6 addresses the social and psychological significance of physical space or 'locale'. Can physical space itself, or indeed space which is designated for certain activities, have general or predictable effects? This is a long-running argument in architectural and town-planning circles and it has been raised recently by widespread criticism of contemporary urban and housing design. Chapter 6 argues that those suggesting that physical space has great effects on social and personal life may well be overestimating the significance of architecture and design. On the other hand, they are also drawing our attention to people's instincts for personal security and possession, demands which have largely gone missing from contemporary urban sociology and which deserve more serious analysis.

Chapter 7 pulls the main themes of the book together into a coherent conceptual framework. Using realist epistemology, it shows how a concern with the 'biotic' or instinctive bases of personal and social life can be combined with an understanding of the social or cultural relations and processes which are more familiar features of contemporary urban sociology. Chapter 7 also suggests that elements of functionalist sociology could well be used in our attempt to combine an understanding of the biotic and social orders. Functionalism suggests that social relations and institutions are, in part at least, organised around the personal instincts and the reproduction of the human species. The book concludes by suggesting that urban studies could be an ideal context for the develop-

ment of a new and unified science. This would combine the insights of
sociology with those of such disciplines as evolutionary biology and
psychology.

Urban sociology emerges as an extraordinarily diverse discipline and
one subject to constant changes of theme. My objective is to begin the
construction of a more robust urban sociology; one which is a more
unified discipline and one which addresses itself to arguments within
sociology itself. One such argument is the long-running debate on the
relationship between structure and agency. 'Structure' is often equated in
the social sciences with deep-lying social structures such as the relationship between capital and wage labour. Here we will be exploring the
proposition that there are other structures affecting human conduct,
specifically those lying deep within people's mental and biological
organisation. We will see how these take the form of demands for self-
esteem and the social value of others; in short the construction of 'moral
careers'.

Broader social structures and processes certainly persist. Indeed, they
are centrally significant in both constraining and enabling the construction of moral careers and the establishment of personal and social
identities. On the other hand, these social structures are always interacting with the structures represented by the organisation of the human mind
and the forms of behaviour to which this organisation leads. Thus the
dualism between structure and agency emerges from this as partly
misplaced. People clearly have the capacity to reflect and act on their own
initiative. Furthermore, social structures (such as those between capital
and labour) are, of course, peculiarly resistant to fundamental change. At
the same time, the extent to which people realise their capacities and the
degree to which social change actually does occur are results of structures
and processes internal to people's psychologies as well as those associated
with society at large.

These themes have a particular significance for urban sociology. The
main problem I will be addressing is what Giddens calls 'time–space
distantiation': the increasing spread of social life across time and space,
combined with the growing concentration of economic and political
power. I explore some of the implications of such centralisation and
globalisation for people's lives. On the one hand, these globally organised
processes mean that most people have a decreasing appreciation of, and
control over, the processes affecting their lives. As a result, daily routines
and practices become detached from the social world and rendered
meaningless. Nevertheless, individuals are not passive. They persist in

asserting their identities during the course of social interaction within the small-scale localities to which their daily lives are inevitably tied.

Urban sociology's core theme is, therefore, central to sociology as a whole. More important still, it is a theme which is central to the human condition. As Georg Simmel wrote in 'The metropolis and mental life' nearly a century ago:

The deepest problems of modern life flow from the attempt of the individual to maintain the independence and individuality of his existence against the sovereign powers of society, against the weight of historical heritage and the external culture and technique of life.[1]

NOTES AND REFERENCES

1. G. Simmel (1971) 'The metropolis and mental life', in D. Levine (ed.), *Georg Simmel on Individuality and Social Forms*, Chicago University Press, Chicago, p. 324. (Originally published 1903.)

1

THE EXPERIENCE OF LOCALITY

REINTRODUCING THE EXPRESSIVE ORDER

This book has been written in response to two closely connected developments. First, urban sociology is in danger of being left behind by events. It is over a quarter of a century now since Jane Jacobs in her *Life and Death of Great American Cities* called for a greater understanding of urban life; one sensitive to the ways in which people actually experienced towns but one which at the same time recognises the powerful economic and political forces affecting urban life and the organisation of cities.[1] Her concerns are increasingly expressed today. The safety of public streets, for example, or the supposed effects of public sector housing design on people's behaviour are still much discussed.[2] More recently, the future king of Britain has been spearheading a popular appeal against large-scale property development destroying old buildings and for people gaining greater control over the design and management of their homes. He has managed to enlist widespread public support.

Urban sociology has not remained entirely immune to these kinds of development. But it is seriously lacking when it comes to understanding how people use, understand and interpret the social and spatial environments of which they are part. This brings us to this book's second concern. In many respects urban sociology has certainly made good progress. As we shall see, it is now providing us with good understandings of broad economic, social and political processes, their unevenness and their impacts on individuals and localities. But how people actually use and experience their social and spatial environments has been largely ignored or dealt with by environmental psychology as a wholly separate exercise.

There are, however, signs that sociology is attempting to deal more systematically with questions of locality and space. Giddens, in particular, attempts to draw a concept of 'locale' into his conceptualisation of how human actions relate to social structures.[3] His starting-point is what he calls 'the duality of structure', the idea that social structures are both the medium and the outcome of human practices and conduct. Human agency comes into this in so far as he insists that people are not cultural dopes of 'mere bearers of a mode of production'.[4] Rather, they have an understanding of the social and spatial environment and actively use this environment in the creation of their own lives and the social systems of which they are part.

A way of summarising Giddens's argument is that society is not aspatial and there cannot be any aspatial sociology. Space cannot be treated as an optional extra if we are attempting to develop a satisfactory understanding of social relations, social processes and their relationships to people as active human beings. We will be building on this essential insight. Nevertheless, Giddens's definition of 'locale' is actually too limiting if we are to develop an adequate spatial sociology. A locale in Giddens's terms is:

[A] physical region involved as the setting of interaction, having definite boundaries which help to concentrate interaction in one way or another.[5]

So a locale for Giddens is very much a physical setting within which human interaction takes place. It is clear he means a physical setting, albeit a *socially defined* setting, which is dedicated or allocated to distinct uses. It is also one which may well be subdivided into smaller, socially defined zones. For Giddens,

[Locales range] from a room in a house, or street corner, the shopfloor of a factory, towns and cities to the territorially demarcated areas occupied by region states. But they are typically internally regionalised.[6]

Physical space thus socially defined may well be very significant in affecting people's lives and their encounters with social relations and processes. Indeed, we will encounter this significance later in this book. On the other hand, we need a stronger notion to encapsulate the idea that people's surroundings (whether the home, the workplace, the town or even the nation) are constituted by social systems. People's daily lives consist most importantly of encountering and interacting with other people. The fact that such encounters take place in designated types of space is important but not central if we are trying to prise out the social significance of people's surroundings. So, in addition to Giddens's locale, we will also use the word 'locality': the latter referring to a local social system, the former to space allocated to certain kinds uf use.

Our objective in seemingly being rather pedantic over points of definition is to evolve a way in which the currently more familiar and better developed parts of urban sociology may be advanced. We do this by linking it with the 'expressive order' – the ways in which people interact with one another, with the physical environment and how they articulate their experiences. Later we will be linking urban sociology to the 'biotic order', this referring to the range of instinctive actions in which people engage. Some of these instincts are indeed shared with other species.

How people interact, relate to one another and express deep-lying instinctive feelings all have considerable implications for the broader social, political and economic relationships in which they are caught up. The dualism between structures and human agency, and the division between two kinds of urban sociology which we have started to discuss here cannot for long be convincingly maintained. This book, by introducing questions of 'locality' and 'locale', represents a first step in overcoming these dualisms. These include not only the relations between structure and agency, but those between people's innate qualities and the social processes of which they are part.

It should be noted here that the question of scale is not the most crucial of issues. We will be trying to develop a general understanding of the role of locale and locality in social change at whatever level of spatial analysis. In Chapter 3, for example, we give some attention to locale and locality at the scale of the workplace. In Chapter 4 we are partly concerned with the scale of the home. The urban scale (roughly, the scale represented by people's everyday lives) does, nevertheless, have a particular social significance. It is important for most people involved in paid work and the use of such resources as shops or schools. A scale somewhere between that of the elderly person and the high-flying executive is the context of most people's daily life.

Localities, and relatively small-scale locales are, then, especially important as the context of people's everyday lives. This brings us to the second point: and, indeed, I wish to argue that this is the key theme or 'problematic' for urban sociology. Everyday lives are, of course, influenced, reproduced and changed by structures of social, economic and political power which spread well beyond our immediate experience and control. Indeed, as Giddens also argues, we can envisage contemporary society as increasingly 'stretched' over time and space. The comparatively self-contained nature of, say, a tribe or a mediaeval village is being increasingly supplanted by a system in which everyday life is affected by international markets and in which decisions are being spatially and temporally removed from the context in which they are eventually experienced.

But this still leaves the question of precisely *how* we understand the relationships between social change and localities, as the contexts of everyday life. Exactly *how* do locality and locale matter? The 'stretching' of social life can lead, Giddens argues, to a condition of 'ontological insecurity', a sense in which people have precious little understanding of the processes affecting their inner selves, their daily lives, the sense of who they are and where they belong.

The sense in which this lack of understanding is evident and the extent to which it can be recovered varies according to the particular kinds of social relations that people are confronting. In the realm of paid work, for example, capital is relatively mobile. This means that if a locality (remembering this consists of a local social system) is seen as non-profitable then capital can and will move elsewhere. In this realm, therefore, social structures remain relatively immune from struggle, resistance and the various forms of 'escape attempt' which people make to regain a sense of self-management and ontological security. There is nevertheless an important tension here. Many people, of course, value employment and find it important in establishing personal and social esteem.

The situation is rather different in social life outside paid work. Here, whether in the home or in the wider realm of consumption, people do seem able to use social structures (in particular the marketplace in which goods and services are exchanged) to gain a greater sense of identity and self-determination. This is not to deny that even in civil society our needs and instincts are to some extent fashioned by advertising agencies, multinational organisations and the particular products that they decide to create for the market. So again we are partly caught up in the deeper workings of industrial economies over which we have precious little direct control. At the same time, however, there is real scope here for choice. Besides, people's lives are not wholly constrained by the items they have chosen. A cooker does not determine what we actually cook, a car does not determine where we actually drive and a home computer does not determine the words we process.

Therefore, in the realm of civil society and consumption there are genuine options and these can be used to establish a sense of personal and social identity. This leads some psychologists and sociologists to see civil society as a prime sphere of self-determination. For some, as we will see, it is the setting of a new 'postmodern' culture in which some people, at least, are increasingly able to carve out a sense of being or 'self'.

The sense in which locality 'matters' is again different when we come to the political sphere. It is sometimes suggested that it is here where locality has its greatest social significance. It is arguably in the political sphere that we see most variability in social relations. This variability underlies, for example, the confrontations between local and national governments which have been one of the major themes of contemporary British society. At an international level, the differences between, say, the USA and the USSR are perhaps greatest in the realm of politics and state strategy. Yet there is another tension here. At one level, an enfranchised individual can affect the nature of her or his society. On the other hand, the same individual is again caught up in extraordinarily subtle but well-entrenched forms of surveillance.

Finally, there is the difficult issue of how physical space and 'locale' relate to society and social change. This matter is pursued in Chapter 6. Physical distances between people and the allocation of physical spaces to certain kinds of activity must indeed have some effects on social processes and social relations. The problem, however, is that it is extremely difficult to generalise about these effects. There is no knowing whether, for example, the creation of a new town physically separate from a metropolis will produce a better or worse life for the residents of either the new town or the metropolis. Again, a wall between two people clearly inhibits (for a while at least) these people's interaction. But it is very difficult to be precise about the effects of such inhibition.

Although I am trained as an architect, I resist physical determinism of the kind still associated with much thinking in architectural and town planning. Physical space is socially constructed. Indeed, we have seen that this is what Giddens is implying when he refers to 'locales'. Spaces are indeed usually socially specified for some kinds of activities. Locales carry social meanings and symbols which are widely accepted and which considerably affect social relations. Even though these meanings and symbols can certainly be challenged and reinterpreted, they still deeply affect how people as individuals and groups interpret their own and other people's circumstances. The language and symbols associated with physical space are part of the 'expressive order' alluded to earlier. Locales are, then, intimately bound up with people's actions and social change. On the other hand, we need to constantly bear in mind that people (and their interpretation or use of locales) are the causal elements in such change. It is still not clear whether locales themselves, as Giddens seems to be suggesting, have systematic and predictable effects on behaviour. Firm evidence is not yet available, although we need to keep an open mind.

Such assertions about the expressive order, the role of locality and of locales are easy enough to make. How, though, can they be systematically introduced into our understanding of society and social change?

LOCALITIES, MORAL CAREERS AND THE EXPRESSIVE ORDER

Fortunately, as should become clear during this and the following chapter, there is a well-established strand in social and psychological analysis which facilitates the creation of a more complete urban sociology. It is one which allows us to recognise in a rigorous way people's own interpretations and theories. Here the work of Erving Goffman and of social psychologists who have developed his work will be invaluable. Nevertheless, much of this work is still insufficiently 'social'. It needs linking to conventional urban sociology with its emphases on structural relations, broad social changes and upheavals.

What does this new kind of urban or spatial sociology entail? Firstly, it certainly involves incorporating many of the insights of existing urban sociology; including those stemming from political economy and an emphasis on broad social relations. In addition to this use of established urban sociology, though, localities are also envisaged as the settings within which face-to-face interactions take place. As regards physical space, or what we are calling 'locale', certain regions tend to be associated with certain kinds of activity and interaction.

Goffman's work has to be the starting-point for this second kind of perspective. He, especially, has given emphasis both to the expressive order and to its spatial implications.[7] He argues that in a social context individuals are constantly communicating with each other, mainly through verbal means but also through such means as non-verbal communication, styles of dress, their homes and the commodities with which they surround themselves. At the same time, individuals are supplying impressions of themselves to others. Meanwhile, these other people are constantly seeking information on those with whom they are interacting; information about that person's status, self-conception and general attitudes. This information indicates how they are expected to relate to the others with whom they are interacting.

Goffman gives considerable emphasis to the spatial contexts in which these interactions take place. Indeed, one of his central points is that human activity is 'regionalised', space being intimately bound up with social and personal life. He uses a dramaturgical or theatrical idea to describe how space is implicated. He distinguishes between 'front regions' for public display and 'back regions' (or, using the theatrical metaphor, 'backstage' areas) not intended for public access.

Goffman thus argues that equivalent to the 'front' performances and 'back' activities in which we all engage are certain kinds of 'front' and 'back' regions which are associated with these kinds of activity. Front regions, he suggests, are where the performance is enacted, where certain codes of acceptable conduct, decorum and etiquette are maintained. It is here that people will go to considerable ends to ensure that their actions and interchanges meet certain socially acceptable standards. Back regions, by contrast, are where the performer can drop her or his front. It is here that the formal speaking of lines can be temporarily abandoned, where self-expression can take place without concerns for obeying predominant norms of social behaviour.

Four additional points need to be made about front and back activities and regions. First, as Goffman constantly reminds us, front and back activities and regions are very much two sides of the same coin. Fronts and backs are mutually dependent upon each other. As Goffman puts it:

Front regions are where a particular performance is or may be in progress, and back regions are where action occurs that is related to the performance but inconsistent with the appearance fostered by the performance.[8]

Secondly, people may well of course be scheduling their activities in such a way to keep up appearances. Employment often entails, for example, one presentation of self while home involves another. Complications and special arrangements for the presentation of self ensue when the two spheres intermesh. The association of back behaviour with back regions and of front with front regions may well need rapid adjustment as, for example, the boss comes to dinner or a spouse visits a partner's place of employment.

This brings us to the third point regarding the relation between activities and regions. Goffman's idea of front and back regions uses a dramaturgical metaphor but this is actually somewhat misleading. There are two points here. Firstly, the same region may double as both a back and a front region. The same locale may well find itself used both for front and back activities. A street or a housing estate may well, for example, be used for front purposes during the day and back purposes under cover of darkness. Similarly, what for some people is a front may at the same time for others be a back. A home may, for example, be a front for a house-proud individual while it is a back for someone returning home tired from work to be him or herself.

This relates to the second point. The 'frontness' or 'backness' of a locale or a form of behaviour is not, as Goffman sometimes seems to suggest, permanent, innate or endemic. Frontness or backness is a result of social and power relations, incorporating as it does the mutual surveillance of some individuals and groups by others. 'Frontness' and 'backness' are socially constructed. As such they need constant revision to deal with resistances, challenges and the crises which individuals face as a result of wider processes such as the concentration of economic and political power. We will discuss this further in later chapters.

The fourth point is important since it raises the crucial issue of how people's understandings and actions relate to wider social structures. This again concerns the social construction of front and back by classes and by other dominant and subordinate groups. It is fair to say that Goffman does refer to the question of how acceptable etiquettes and codes of behaviour are actually established. His concerns remain, however, at the micro level – with the relatively small number of people which an individual confronts during her or his life. Goffman contrasts, for example, the different forms of treatment given to patients in public and private hospitals. Those who are able to afford private treatment are often able to protect their own privacy and 'self' through separate rooms or screens. Low income people may find their personal and spatial identities frequently transgressed, privacy only being obtained in the terminal stages of an illness. What he does not discuss, however, are the wider processes affecting how, indeed whether, public or private health resources are made available.

We will later be using and developing these ideas as a means of understanding people's actions (and in particular the sustaining of human identity) in social and physical settings. But, before elaborating on these ideas, we need to remind ourselves of how Goffman and later authors actually use them to create an understanding of individuals and the social world.

The emphasis on front and back activities (though less the emphasis on front and back regions) is reflected in Goffman's work on closed institutions. These include the hospital discussed above and also asylums and prisons. One of Goffman's main concerns here is with what he calls 'moral careers'. These are the more-or-less regular and standard sequences of change to the lives of certain classes of individuals. These moral careers are strongly influenced by formal structures (including career structures) incorporated into organisations such as state institutions and private companies.

For Goffman, though, the main point about moral careers is that they are the result of how people conceive of themselves and of how others (including those of higher or lower status) conceive of them. The result of these moral valuations is a moral career, a generalisable form of social progression and mobility. A key point about such moral careers is that they cannot be understood simply by examining purely formal structures and rules such as those associated with institutions. An understanding entails examining the expressive order: the language, concepts and values which people themselves use in their expression of self and in their evaluation of others.

The work of what Rom Harré calls 'the new psychology' has some close similarities to that of Goffman.[9] It is an attempt to construct a genuinely *social* psychology; one recognising that, while people are caught up in social structures constraining and enabling their actions, individuals are also active and reflective; creating their own lives in relation to others.

This latter approach entails two important distinctions. Firstly, there is what Harré calls the 'practical order'; the basic processes of surviving and biological reproduction. Secondly, there is the expressive order; that aspect of personal and social life concerned with the construction of self and personal esteem. Harré, therefore, distinguishes between what he calls the 'practical aspects of activity' which he sees as 'directed to material and biological ends' and the 'expressive aspects of activity' which are 'directed to ends such as the presentation of the self as rational and worthy of respect'.[10]

His approach to the understanding of human agency therefore involves combining an understanding of both these aspects of personal life. Harré nevertheless believes that in contemporary Western society the expressive order has a special significance. Again echoing Goffman, he argues that the dominant preoccupation of human social life is the acquisition and maintenance of recognition, honour and reputation in other people's eyes.

This special emphasis on the expressive order leads Harré to give special prominence to Veblen, the sociologist of middle class mores in early twentieth century America.[11] Giving great attention to civil society, Veblen argued that the acquisition of property and status was the characteristic feature of advanced industrial, especially American, society. 'Accumulated property', he argued, 'more and more replaces trophies of predatory exploit as the conventional exponent of prepotence and success.'[12] Veblen suggested that this emphasis on property and status symbols stems from the emergence and growing influence of a 'leisure class' whose social arrival was being signalled by various forms of conspicuous consumption and spectacular uses of leisure time. Furthermore, this class of people was to a large extent setting the social pace for the 'lower' classes of society; even those who in fact had precious little leisure time in which to display their increasing spending power.

So, adopting Veblen's emphasis on the expressive order, Harré argues that: 'for most people at most times the expressive order dominates or shapes the practical order'.[13] Harré becomes especially concerned here with what he calls 'architectonic man'. This means that all types of people are actively engaged in creating language, objects and theories representing and making sense of their experience of social structures and processes. Such symbols and interpretations are not, of course, simply *ex*pressions of individuals' selves. They inform people's actions (which in turn affects the social structures and processes of which they are part) and they supply *im*pressions which are interpreted and acted on by other members of society.

The basic points about the 'new psychology' are that society is constructed by active people and that people as individuals are largely constructed *by* society. As such, it relates closely to symbolic interactionism: a form of analysis which envisages social structures as the product of the individual's socialisation and the roles that he or she adopts. As we see in Chapter 2, this line of thinking had its origins in the Chicago School of Sociology, and especially in the writings of G. H. Mead. The form of interaction to which Harré and his colleagues attribute central importance is conversation. This normally entails, of course, a physical setting in which face-to-face exchanges take place. Harré *et al.* hypothesise (see Figure 1.1) that the direction of influence on an individual's conscious-

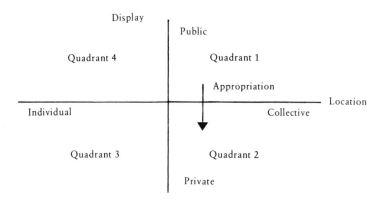

Figure 1.1 The true 'space' of psychology. (From R. Harré, D. Clarke and N. DeCarlo, *Motives and Mechanisms*, Methuen, London, 1985. Reproduced with permission.)

ness and 'display' (in the form of language and other forms of communication) is from the public and collective towards the individual, even though this is clearly a circular process with individual consciousness and language feeding back to the public and collective level. The direction of influence on a person's psychology is therefore from quadrants 1, 2, 3, 4, etc. To put this in a form relevant to our central concerns, individuals encountering each other in locales and localities are constantly 'appropriating' part of the public discourse, making it into their own personal discourse and individual identities, perhaps suppressing their feelings when confronted with opposing or apparently superior knowledge.

To link this to our earlier discussion of locality and locale, we find individual consciousness, language and social identity interacting in a dialectical fashion with the immediate social context of people's lives. Harré *et al.* are, however, arguing that the main direction of influence tends to be from collective understandings and language, with individuals appropriating parts of the communal discourse towards their own ends. This analysis is based on the work of Lev Vygotsky, a renowned Russian developmental psychologist. It is a rigorous way of arguing how people's mental processes are simultaneously shaped by their social environment while they are at the same time, albeit in a weaker way, contributing to that same environment themselves.

Harré *et al.*'s work is a critique of much current psychology. One of

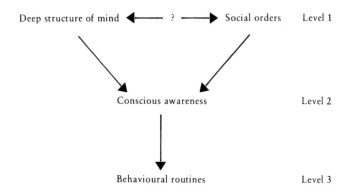

Deep structure of mind ◄——— ? ———► Social orders   Level 1

Conscious awareness   Level 2

Behavioural routines   Level 3

Figure 1.2 Levels of the mind's control hierarchy. (From R. Harré, D. Clarke and
N. DeCarlo, *Motives and Mechanisms*, Methuen, London, 1985. Reproduced
with permission.)

psychology's main problems has long been a special emphasis on the
individual and an implicit assumption that society is not in fact social but
is made up of individuals whose actions stem only from internal
psychological or biological mechanisms. Harré *et al.*'s approach suggests,
by contrast, psychological mechanisms are only fully realised in social
contexts; those of, say, the family or the company.

This new emphasis in psychology on people as *social* beings leads Harré
et al. to propose a framework for the understanding of human agency as
simultaneously made by and making society. Figure 1.2 represents Harré
et al.'s view of the structures and processes affecting the human mind.

The structures and processes are arranged hierarchically. At the top are
two relatively distinct sets of structures and processes governing in a
broad strategic manner the actions of individuals and societies. On the
one hand, this level consists, according to Harré *et al.*, of the 'seething
networks of social relations in which we are embedded'.[14] These are,
however, seen as responsive both to the deep-rooted emotional structures
at this higher level and to the lower levels of the human mind.
Furthermore, they are variable over space and time. As regards the 'deep
structures of the human mind' at the highest level, Harré *et al.* appear to
be alluding to Jungian psychology. This suggests that people's actions are
subconsciously monitored and governed by a range of primordial
archetypes, images and emotions which have evolved as man has emerged

from an animal state. It has been constructed by the very basic themes of human life: birth, death, control and survival and parenthood.

A key point to note is that this approach envisages the human mind as largely constructed by social or collective processes. The mind is also seen as regulating much of human action. Nevertheless, it is a level not readily accessible other than through special psychoanalytic procedures such as dream analysis and hypnosis.

The middle level of the brain's hierarchy is the most important for the 'new psychology'. This is what Harré *et al.* call the 'information-rich level of decision'.[15] It is here that our conscious awareness is located and here that we exercise a degree of knowledge of, and control over, our actions. It is 'the middle manager' of the mind, monitoring and controlling those processes and relationships over which we have little understanding or control. It is important to remember here the insistence, outlined earlier, that individual actions and consciousness both affect social structures and are affected by them. Conversation, language and communication are the defining characteristics of this level. And these different forms of symbolic interaction are simultaneously making and changing society, *while at the same time* constructing the individuals engaging in these social and collective activities.

The lowest level is also envisaged as connected to the other two levels of the hierarchy. It is also the level which, through cognitive psychology, is best understood by psychological theory. This is the level at which individual organisms experience and respond in a virtually automatic way to their physical and social environment. Raising the voice to make oneself heard is an example.

Given this hierarchy, language, conversation and communication at the middle level become the raw material for understanding how individuals simultaneously construct both their selves and the social world. It is at this point that Harré *et al.*'s work can be related back to that of Goffman outlined earlier. A central objective of examining people's own concepts, language and understandings is again to understand the 'moral career', this being in Harré's words:

[A] history of an individual person with respect to the attitudes and beliefs that others have of him and the attitudes and beliefs about himself that he forms on the basis of his readings of the attitudes and beliefs of others.[16]

The hope is, of course, that moral careers are not simply biographies of individuals. Both Harré *et al.*'s aims, and those of Goffman, are to trace typical moral career-patterns. Harré envisages such generality as partly reflecting broad underlying psychological mechanisms such as the Jungian archetypes.

For these microsociologists and social psychologists this special concern with moral careers stems from the fact that there is often a systematic difference between the opinions which an individual may hold about her- or himself and the views held by others. A large part of social change (though, as we will discuss later, by no means all) is seen as stemming from this tension.

We started earlier to discuss how 'locale' or 'locality' fits into all this. Harré, like Goffman, sees all these processes and interactions taking place in social and physical environments. Going beyond this, individual behaviour is again not envisaged as taking place within pre-set social circumstances. Rather, it is actively making and changing these circumstances as individuals assign meanings to one another's expressions and act accordingly.

Harré's approach to space has close similarities with that of Goffman. The meaning of the built environment is seen as socially constructed. On the one hand, sets of physical symbols indicate what locales are to be used for. On the other, locales are also a context of tension and potential conflict as individuals and social groups each try to assert their personal and social identities.

Just as each species of animal has its own spatial environment, in every given area each category of people, professions and sexes, families and age groups, have different spaces within which they freely move, all, for example, within the one city. Each has some spaces proper to itself alone.[17]

The tensions stem from the fact that what Harré calls the 'low status person' is in many circumstances exposed in what Goffman would call a 'front region', his or her activities being under continual threat of supervision. Meanwhile, as we discuss in considerably more detail in Chapter 5, the activities of supervisors, managers or senior bureaucrats are frequently hidden from view and supervision. In short, the expressive order is being acted out in locales and localities with sets of individuals in different status and class circumstances asserting and protecting their identities through the assertion and protection of territory.

Regarding what we have earlier termed 'locality', Harré makes the crucial point that the system of rules and values underlying the expressive order may well vary considerably over space. As a result, the forms of typical moral careers may themselves vary according to the particular local circumstances in which they are being acted out. In some localities the practical order (incorporating questions of class and material questions of sheer survival) may well remain more significant to social and individual life than questions of status and the expressive order.

Furthermore, the form of the expressive order can also be expected to vary between localities. As Urry's work implies, we should examine the expressive order in relation to the forms of class and property relations specific to a particular region. In some regions, relations of class (capital and labour) still dominate local social and community life. In an increasing number of localities, however, other kinds of relation are beginning to dominate people's relationships and politics. These are the 'horizontal' relations Urry writes of; those of, for example, gender, race, religion and domestic property. The middle classes will tend to act as reference groups for 'lower' social classes living in the area in question. Nevertheless, the precise form of such influence can be expected to vary according the precise nature of local elites.[18]

To sum up here, Goffman and Harré *et al.*'s central contribution, as well as that of Giddens (who himself makes extensive use of Goffman) is to insist on individuals as conscious, decision making human agents. They are, nevertheless, acting within social and spatial contexts and partly guided by underlying psychological mechanisms. These authors are intent on understanding people's own accounts of the social world and on the ways in which physical and social space is implicated in the development of moral careers. However, as these authors do indeed suggest, there is a tension here. An individual's account and understanding of the social world constantly runs up against the harsh objective facts of social change. It is constantly 'tested' against the actual social circumstances which she or he is attempting to understand. This brings us to some difficulties with Goffman's and Harré's framework.

SOME PROBLEMS WITH THE GOFFMAN AND HARRÉ FRAMEWORK

Three particular problems can be mentioned here. First, there are some inherent difficulties in the very literal application of a dramaturgical metaphor to social life. Giddens makes a similar point when he suggests that it may be a considerable oversimplification to imply that the whole of social life consists of people putting up façades in order to maintain their social and self esteem. Those who do hold to the belief that the whole of social life is simply a series of 'security operations' intended to protect their identities may well, as Giddens puts it, 'display modes of anxiety of an extreme kind'.[19]

Giddens's point is largely based on a reading of contemporary social psychology and psychiatry. Especially important here is R. D. Laing who, in his discussion of 'the divided self', suggests that much of everyday social life consists of people creating and presenting selves which are disembodied from their actual being.[20] These selves can be seen as what we have earlier called 'escape attempts'; means of creating individual and social identity in a society which is seen as threatening. But, whereas these forms of personal alienation and presentation of false selves may be a regular and relatively harmless feature of most people's lives, they of course become highly problematic if taken to extremes. Laing is suggesting that 'the divided self' is indeed a general condition of alienation in contemporary life. His main concern, though, is with schizophrenia, where the schism between self and body is considerable and a regular part of someone's life.

Back regions are not simply where back (or low social esteem) activities take place. They are also the settings in which tension and conflict can occur. As Giddens puts it:

Back regions clearly often do form a significant resource which both the powerful and the less powerful can utilise reflexively to sustain a psychological distancing between their own interpretations of social processes and those enjoined by 'official' norms.[21]

Despite, however, the obvious differences between theatre and real social life, the dramaturgical metaphor is still valuable. It needs, however, adapting to recognise more complexity. As suggested earlier in relation to Giddens's work, the ways in which people present themselves to others do indeed obey certain tacit rules. Locales, with their symbolic boundaries and architectural forms indicating appropriate types of behaviour within their confines, are systematically bound up with the expressive order; the ways in which people present themselves to each other. Nevertheless, what is front or back behaviour and how locales and localities are bound up with this behaviour is socially constructed and interpreted. Again, it is a matter of introducing social relations between classes, genders, gene-rations and holders and non-holders of state power.

This brings us to the point about front and back regions which is not adequately recognised by either Goffman or Giddens and which we have discussed earlier. The same region can simultaneously be both front *and* back. These qualities are negotiated, the extent of their backness and frontness depending on the relationships and interpretations of those using them. But we can go further than this. There is a strong sense, as we will see the Chicago School of Urban Sociology arguing, in which the *dominant* view of a particular region is that associated with dominant social classes. In contemporary, developed society this particularly refers to white, middle class, middle aged males.

This comment on the social basis of front and back brings us to the second point about Goffman and Harré. Their special emphasis is on the expressive order and the tacit assumption (partly stemming from Veblen) that culture filters 'down' from the dominant social orders to the lower social reaches. This is indeed a reasonable first attempt to gain an understanding of who or what defines what front or back behaviours and regions actually are. But, as recent work on cultural forms suggest, the processes by which cultures are formed and lived are actually more problematic and conflict-ridden than this. This is suggested by, for example, Bourdieu's work on cultural relations in France.[22] It also comes through very clearly in work by the Centre for Contemporary Cultural Studies.[23] Working class ways of life can actually be seen as quite distinct from those of the middle classes. According to Bourdieu, working class ways of life remain largely organised around the 'practical order' of simply getting by. For the dominant classes, by contrast:

What is rare and constitutes an inaccessible luxury or an absurd fantasy for those at an earlier or lower level becomes banal and common, and is relegated to the order of the taken-for-granted by the appearance of new, rarer and more distinct goods.[24]

So, according to Bourdieu, the practical order is, for some people at least, still alive and well. Furthermore, forms of distinction are not simply passed 'down' from the dominant social orders. Elites may well acquire status and identity by adopting (and adapting) ways of life led by working class people. Similarly, as work of the Centre for Contemporary Cultural Studies argues, youth cultures distinguish themselves by partly adopting the very lifestyles (cars, clothes and so forth) of the more affluent. Goffman and Harré may well be right in asserting that the cultural forms adopted by economically, politically and socially dominant groups tend to dominate those adopted by others. But the general point is that the distinguishing symbols and cultural forms adopted by different social groups are, to a greater extent than either Goffman or Harré suggest, a result of struggle and conflict.

The third problem with Goffman's framework (but to a lesser extent with that of Harré) is that the world where they see moral careers are being carved out is still not sufficiently social and political. In short, there are again deep-lying, persistent social structures which both constrain and enable people's presentation of self.

How, for example, should we explain the growth of the middle classes in contemporary advanced industrial societies? This is a social group which is particularly important to these authors. Part of such growth can, of course, be attributed, as Goffman and Harré imply, to their sustained, systematic and largely successful search for self-esteem and status. But such a generalised and long-term development is also linked to broader structural changes which cannot be simply understood as resulting from the actions of the individuals. Factory automation and labour-process deskilling are, for example, having a systematically polarising effect; creating highly qualified mental labourers on the one hand and unskilled or semi-skilled workers on the other.

The third point is, in short, that there is still missing in much of Goffman's and Harré *et al.*'s analysis the sense of society as constituted by structures and processes operating partly independent of the actions of individuals and the microrelations of social groups. Social change and upheaval, as we have seen earlier, affect the 'expressive orders' people use and their interpretations and understandings of themselves and of the social world. But the continuing concentration on the individual (albeit the individual as socially constructed and engaging in social life) will not allow us adequately to understand the circumstances under which expressive orders are formed and changed.

There is, nevertheless, work which allows us to make the necessary connections between social change, structural upheaval and the expressive order. We will be encountering it throughout the following chapters. Furthermore, this work illuminates our special concerns with locale and locality.[25]

LOCALITIES, LOCALES, MORAL CAREERS AND THE EXPRESSIVE ORDER: SOME LITERARY ILLUSTRATIONS

Novels and fictional literature provide some of the best insights into the ways notions of 'country' and 'city' are used in language to express deep-rooted instincts and their relationships to fundamental social change. They also illustrate the ways in which cities are the context of human association and the formation of moral careers.

As regards the city and the expressive order, consider Raymond Williams's *The Country and the City*.[26] This study of British poetry and fiction over a period of some two hundred years demonstrates particularly well how social change has been consistently linked to changing forms of consciousness. The key point to Williams's book is the idea that country and city are frequently used to explain and understand profoundly unsettling social and political change. Language, or the expressive order, is directly responsive to crisis and upheaval, with people searching for personal identity and a sense of community in order to make sense of their circumstances. As Williams put it:

Wordsworth saw that when we became uncertain in a world of apparent strangers who yet, decisively, have common effect on us, and when forces that will alter our lives are moving all around us in apparently external and unrecognisable forms, we can retreat, for security, into a deep subjectivity, or we can look around us for social pictures, social signs, social messages, to which characteristically, we try to relate as individuals but so as to discover, in some form, community.[27]

So, according to Williams, the language of 'country' and 'city' is widely used as a means by which people attempt to explain, understand and escape from the circumstances of their lives. These include alienation, detachment and the division between mental and manual labour in contemporary social life. Country and city language of course brings with it a number of other associations. Country is associated with 'directness, connection and mutuality'. City is frequently linked to sophistication and a relatively impersonal life.[28]

But it is important to recognise that such language and associations are not simply forms of expression articulating alternative societies and ways of life. They may well reflect the real experiences of small communities and large cities. As such, they frequently inform people's actions. Moving to the country may well entail actually moving to a more direct form of personal, face-to-face, form of community: one in which personal identity can be found through immediate association. Moving to the city is indeed an effective means of keeping up with emergent ways of life. Contemporary urban social theory consistently denies the explanatory significance of 'the urban' and 'the rural' in people's understandings and discourse. But the expressive categories 'urban' and 'rural' help us connect changes in the social world with changes in people's consciousness and action.[29]

Williams's emphasis on city and country and on the expressive order ties in usefully with sociological work which is more closely linked to that of Goffman discussed earlier. Giddens refers to the stretching of social systems across time and space as 'time–space distantiation'; the implication being that contemporary societies are held together by world markets, bureaucracies and massive political concentrations rather than by plans and strategies formed through direct face-to-face relations.

Again, however, major social upheavals can generate profoundly unsettling effects on consciousness. Such effects are associated, according to Giddens, with 'ontological insecurity'; a term, as we have seen, referring to the sense of not knowing who, what or even where you are. In these circumstances, the flight to an alternative imagined way of life in 'the city' or 'the country' are further examples of 'escape attempts'; the regular, often quite unremarkable, ways in which people distance themselves from a world they find difficult to understand and try to establish zones of autonomy and self-management.[30] Notions of country and city are again, therefore, important means by which individuals can build up relatively stable constructions both of the world and of their own existence within it. On the basis of such understandings they can take action. Again, creative literature helps us explore these links.

Locales, localities and the novel of working class mobility

These images and forms of understanding inform people's 'life plans' and what Goffman would call their 'moral careers'. As both Harré and Goffman suggest, the understanding of moral careers is perhaps best made through conversation and discourse. Again, fictional literature can throw an especially useful light on such careers and their links to social and spatial settings. A second example here is the novel of working class life written in the immediate postwar context of growing material prosperity and the relatively easy mobility of working class people into white collar work. As Laing has described in some detail, much of that era's celebrated literature of contemporary working class life (for example, Amis's *Lucky Jim*, Wain's *Hurry on Down*, Braine's *Room at the Top*, Waterhouse's *Billy Liar*) is centred on 'the young male hero on the make in the fluid situation of a new 1960s Britain'.[31] Crucially, the 'back region' characteristics which these authors associated with the old communities and 'front region' features which they linked to London and the new owner-occupied estates meant that these symbols were made to stand for the old and new ways of life. This is particularly the case for Billy Liar. As Laing argues, there may be a strong sense of Waterhouse's own preferred moral career in his novel:

Billy Liar particularly asserted the urgent need to break out of the northern provincial community if the aspirant individual was to find fulfilment. Billy's particular aspiration (to be a writer) implied that this need might be as pressing for novelists themselves as for their fictional heroes.[32]

Locales, localities and the novel: The hyper-mobile service class

During the late 1980s there has emerged a genre of novels equivalent to those describing the life and times of the upwardly mobile individuals of the 1950s. The 1980s' heroes are also spatially mobile, although this now entails jetting between nations rather than between regions. Unlike the working class heroes of the 1950s, however, these tend to be people who have already 'arrived'. The novels are largely about the anxieties and rewards of being rich in a major city rather than the problems of becoming socially established. Nevertheless, despite the fact that Williams did not assess these later novels, themes similar to those that he identified recur. The city is simultaneously a place of great danger and of opportunity. The country is socially backward but is nevertheless a place of rest and tranquillity. Furthermore, and in line with the concepts advanced by Goffman, Harré and Giddens, the principal drive also affecting these people's lives is the establishment of moral careers; self-esteem as well as the respect of others.

Collectively these are people who Tom Wolfe in *The Bonfire of the Vanities* calls 'The Masters of the Universe'.[33] Wolfe's book is about these people's everyday lives in New York; indulging themselves in every known form of hedonism offered by the city while at the same time trying to insulate themselves from violent threats to life and limb which the great city also brings. The back cover sets the tone:

Sherman McCoy, Wall Street bond-trader with a salary like a telephone number . . . Peter Fallow, expatriate Fleet Street gossip-writer whose price is a free lunch . . . Larry Kramer, assistant DA with a lustful eye on the juror wearing brown lipstick . . . Reverend Reggie Bacon, charismatic ghetto warlord, con-man and power in the streets. . . .

The Bonfire of the Vanities welds their stories together on a night in the Bronx when a $48,000 Mercedes hits a street it shouldn't have been near with a girl in its tan leather bucket seat who shouldn't have been there at all. The next day a young black accident victim is in hospital in a coma and Sherman McCoy has booked himself a one-way ticket to disaster.

Two other recent novels make a point of exploring moral careers and experiences of country and city for 'the masters of the universe'. One is Amis's *Money*, 'a story', according to the front cover, 'of urban excess'.[34] The back cover portrays its hero, John Self, in the following way:

John Self is addicted – to the twentieth century. Porn freak and jetsetter, *aficionado* of wealth and women, Self is the shameless heir to a fast-food culture where money beats out an insistent invitation to futile self-gratification. Out in New York, mingling with the mighty, making a fortune but spending more, Self is embroiled in the corruption, the brutality and the obscenity of the money conspiracy.

Henderson Dores in Boyd's novel *Stars and Bars* is a rather different character, even though he is another hyper-mobile jet setter also desperately seeking social and personal credibility.[35] Once more, the cover is indicative:

Well dressed, quite handsome, unfailingly polite and charming, who would guess Henderson Dores has a guilty secret. . . .

Underneath his gentle English diffidence burns the canker of shyness, and New York, where he now is, is no place for a shrinking violet. Clearly, Henderson must get his head round his problem.

In more strictly academic terms, all these 'Masters of the Universe' are extremely well-off, senior white collar, 'service class' individuals; even though Self is involved in pornography and many other forms of corruption while Henderson makes large amounts of money through his more legitimate job in the commercial art market. They are both fairly young and desperately seeking privileges and position. These are being achieved through rampant and often ruthless individualism.

They are locked in to what Self calls a 'star-spangled lifestyle – London–New York, New York–London'. Their problems stem from their attempt to maintain this lifestyle and culture in the context of New York. For the individuals involved, the contradictions and tensions involved in living cheek-by-jowl with subordinate cultures is a source of great excitement and stimulation. As Self puts it while musing during one of his brief stays in Manhattan:

Now you've seen me in New York before, and you know how I am out here. I wonder what it is: something to do with the energy, the electricity of the place, all the hustle and razz – it fills me with that get up and go. I'm a different proposition in New York, pulled together, really on the ball.[36]

For Henderson too, New York is stimulation. But he has come to New York largely to escape from himself. If Self has a problem of rampant and unconstrained sexuality, Henderson's problem is that of suppressed sexuality:

Henderson has a complaint, a grudge, a grumble of a deep and insidious kind. He doesn't like himself anymore; isn't happy with the personality he's been provided with, thank you very much. Something about him isn't up to scratch, won't do. He'll keep the flesh, but he'd like to do a deal on the spirit, if nobody minds. He wants to change – he wants to be different from what he is. And that, really, is why he is here.[37]

But New York, as well as being a source of stimulation and escape is again a threat for these high-living individuals. Sometimes, as in Henderson's case, the threat is partly paranoia, innocent people returning his lost wallet being seen by him as incipient muggers and appropriately beaten up. Between threats (real and just as often imagined) Henderson nevertheless dreams of the peace of his homeland and autumn in the English Cotswolds. However, New York brings real daily confrontations with the underclasses. For Self (as well as Sherman McCoy in *The Bonfire of the Vanities*) New York is also a jungle of snares and traps which threaten to bring down its residents and visitors in violence. Self's very money and attempts at instant self-gratification leave him and his class feeling prone to periodic muggings.

In the end, the attempt by these economically successful people to lead a lifestyle in which they can both respect themselves and maintain the respect of others with whom they work and live starts to fall apart. Their attempt to spread their lives over too many places and too many people brings, for a while at least, considerable financial success. At the same time, living in a front region such as New York also brings with it violence, robbery, disastrously superficial personal relations and, ultimately, an urgent need to escape from the very escape attempts of their high-flying lifestyle. Giddens's 'time–space distantiation' finally catches up with them and they must escape if they are to avoid being destroyed. Significantly, however, such escape is primarily in the sphere of 'civil society', the sphere of social life outside employment.

An alternative perspective

The 1950s' and 1980s' novels envisage escape and the reconstruction of identity as taking place through spatial mobility and retreat from collective life. But in direct contrast to this formulation, Raymond Williams's own novels offered an alternative solution. Salvation here does not take the form of escape, and certainly not from back to front regions as advanced by the 1950s' genre. For Williams the problem was not to explore separate worlds of old community and of individual 'escape attempts' but to attempt a form of fiction which incorporated an account 'both of the internally seen working class community and of movement of people, still feeling their family and political connections, out of it.'[38]

The objective here, then, was to challenge what he saw as class-based 'back' and 'front' definitions of localities. Rather, his objective was to provide an account of whole societies, including the contradictions and the often conflicting class relations actually experienced by people. As Laing points out, the novel *Border Country* is organised around the geographical separation between two worlds, but its main theme is how these impact on the same individual's life experience.

[This novel] contrasts both the past (from the early 1920s) and the present, different ways of life (the working class loyalist, the university-educated son and the successful small businessman) through Matthew Price's return to his roots to visit his dying father.[39]

Second Generation, however, explored 'contrasting worlds within the same city'.[40] Not only did it explore the relationships between classes and social groups within the same locality but also, through the figure of Kate, the competing household, sexual and political demands made of a single person.

In sum, Williams's novels are less those of escape. In so far as they deal with social and spatial mobility they are exploring the ways that people try to live out the tensions involved. Of special importance to us are these novels' recognition of the complex combinations of instincts and social relations which working and living in a locality necessarily entail.

SUMMARY: LOCALITY, SOCIETY AND THE EXPRESSIVE ORDER

This chapter argues that there is a dimension to spatial or urban sociology which has largely gone missing from recent work. This is the 'expressive order'; how people in face-to-face contact understand society and themselves and express their feelings to others. We adopt a number of concepts to remedy this situation. One is the notion of 'front' and 'back', referring to the socially defined ways in which activities and places are understood. Another is that of 'moral careers', referring to people's attempts to construct a sense of esteem in their own and other people's eyes. Finally, we refer to the concept of 'ontological security': the sense of personal niche, identity and belonging which people seek as social relations and markets are stretched over time and space and as political power becomes increasingly concentrated.

Novelists, who perhaps feel freer than social scientists to explore the realm of the expressive order, provide an initial illustration of how these concepts interconnect. To evolve a more systematic understanding of how people's perceptions of their circumstances are developed we need fully to appreciate the social relations in which they are caught up. These include the relations of class, gender, race and property; and urban sociology has made great strides in this respect. The expressive order also needs to incorporate an understanding of the 'biotic' order: the biological and emotional processes deeply embedded in people's nature. These not only affect individuals but social and political relations. We have so far, however, given relatively little attention to the biotic order. This can best be approached through a re-examination of urban sociology's origins. We will also find that the biotic order has been given substantial consideration since the days of the Chicago School of Urban Sociology.

NOTES AND REFERENCES

1. J. Jacobs (1969) *The Death and Life of Great American Cities,* Vintage, New York.
2. See, for example, A. Coleman (1985) *Utopia on Trial,* Hilary Shipman, London. This is further discussed in Chapter 6.
3. On Giddens's concepts of 'locale' and 'duality of structure' see, in particular, *The Constitution of Society,* Polity, Oxford, 1984.

4. A. Giddens (1979) *Central Problems in Social Theory*, Macmillan, London.

5. A. Giddens (1984) op. cit., p. 375.

6. A. Giddens (1984) op. cit., p. 118.

7. E. Goffman (1971a) *Relations in Public*, Harper & Row, New York; E. Goffman (1971b) *The Presentation of Self in Everyday Life*, Pelican, Harmondsworth; E. Goffman (1968) *Asylums*, Pelican, Harmondsworth.

8. E. Goffman (1971b) op. cit., p. 135.

9. R. Harré (1979) *Social Being. A Theory for Social Psychology*, Blackwell, Oxford; R. Harré, D. Clarke and N. DeCarlo (1985) *Motives and Mechanisms*, Methuen, London; P. Marsh *et al.* (1978) *The Rules of Disorder*, Routledge, London.

10. R. Harré (1979) ibid., p. 19.

11. T. Veblen (1925) *The Theory of the Leisure Class*, Allen & Unwin, London.

12. T. Veblen (1925) ibid., p. 28.

13. T. Veblen (1925) ibid., p. 5.

14. R. Harré *et al.* (1985) op. cit., p. 36.

15. R. Harré (1979) op. cit., p. 27.

16. R. Harré (1979) op. cit. p. 313.

17. R. Harré (1979) ibid., p. 193.

18. On varying forms of local bourgeoisie acting as reference groups for the working class and resulting variations in local class consciousness see in particular J. Foster (1974) *Class Struggle and the Industrial Revolution*, Methuen, London. As regards 'vertical' and 'horizontal' civil societies, the first refers to societies organised around class (capital and wage labour) and the second around other social axes such as housing tenure or race. See J. Urry 'Some themes in the analysis of the anatomy of capitalist societies', *Acta Sociologica*, 25, 4: 405–18.

19. A. Giddens (1984) op. cit., p. 125.

20. R. D. Laing (1965) *The Divided Self*, Pelican, Harmondsworth.

21. A. Giddens (1984) op. cit., p. 126.

22. P. Bourdieu (1984) *Distinction*, Routledge, London.

23. See, for example, J. Clarke, S. Hall, T. Jefferson and B. Roberts (1977) 'Subcultures, cultures and class', in S. Hall and T. Jefferson (eds) *Resistance through Rituals*, Hutchinson, London. For a review of this and related literature, S. Cohen (1980) *Folk Devils and Moral Panics*, Blackwell, London.

24. P. Bourdieu (1984) op. cit., p. 247.

25. A good historical illustration of localities and physical spaces as settings for face-to-face interactions but subject to wider processes and constraints comes in Bohstedt's work on riots and community politics in late eighteenth century England and Wales (J. Bohstedt (1984) *Riots and Community Politics in England and Wales, 1790–1810*, Harvard UP, Cambridge). The context for a number of upheavals and disturbances in this era was food

running out, grain being exported beyond the region it was grown in in search of higher returns, and prices rapidly rising. Here is Bohstedt's account of a 'characteristic' riot in Barrow. On the one hand, it is extremely sensitive to locality, face-to-face familiarity and to the social symbolism of locale. On the other, it demonstrates well how immediate relationships can be constantly subject to external influence and control.

> The rioters deliberately made their interception of grain a *public* act. They seized the high ground politically and even literally, for the churchyard where the crowd stood was four feet above the road where the cavalry stood, and that not only 'equalized' them physically but also added to the Yeomanry's anxiety. The crowd *appropriated* the public centre of the parish, the church, to underscore and perhaps to 'sanctify' the legitimacy of their actions. . . . By drawing in the members of the community the rioters transformed their formally illegal seizure into a public act rendered intelligible and tolerable by the mutual familiarity of the parties (rioters, magistrates and middle-rank mediators) and by the familiarity of their actions, claims and roles. But if a fragile consensus was viable in the local environment, it withered in the harsh light of external definitions of property, order and force. (p. 3)

26. R. Williams (1973) *The Country and the City*, Chatto & Windus, London.
27. R. Williams (1973) ibid., p. 295.
28. R. Williams (1973) ibid., p. 298.
29. For a discussion see A. Sayer (1984) 'Defining the urban', *GeoJournal*, 9: 279–85.
30. The concept of 'escape attempts' came from the 1976 book of that name by S. Cohen and L. Taylor (Allen Lane, London).
31. S. Laing (1986) *Representations of Working Class Life 1957–1964*, Macmillan, London.
32. S. Laing (1986) ibid., p. 77.
33. T. Wolfe (1988) *The Bonfire of the Vanities*, Picador, London.
34. M. Amis (1985) *Money*, Penguin, Harmondsworth.
35. W. Boyd (1985) *Stars and Bars*, Penguin, Harmondsworth.
36. W. Boyd (1985) ibid., p. 96.
37. W. Boyd (1985) ibid., p. 11.
38. R. Williams (1979) *Politics and Letters*, New Left Books, London, p. 272. Quoted in S. Laing (1986) op. cit.
39. S. Laing (1986) op. cit. p. 78.
40. R. Williams (1979) op. cit., p. 285. Quoted in S. Laing (1986) op. cit.

2

RECONSTRUCTING URBAN SOCIOLOGY

In the last chapter we assembled some basic ingredients of a sociology which is more sensitive to people's experience of locality and locale. Four particular, and linked, themes emerged. The first was an increased concern with human association: face-to-face relations between people, and changes to those relations stemming both from underlying instincts and from broader social or 'cultural' processes. The second was locale: a physical setting which is socially defined for front and back activities. The third was moral careers. This refers to people's progress through life: a result both of their attempts to maintain personal esteem and, at the same time, social respect deriving from other people's evaluations. A moral career, in Harré's terms, is:

[The] social history of a person with respect to the attitudes of respect and contempt that others have of him and of his understandings of these attitudes. The attitudes are realised and represented in institutionalised and ritualised forms in which respect and contempt are tested and meted out in particular societies.[1]

Finally, I have argued that urban sociology's key concern is the division between everyday life being led in small-scale localities and the fact that social relations and processes are increasingly organised at a global level.

As a way of understanding these linked themes we have argued for an increased emphasis on 'the expressive order': the understandings, interpretations and theories which people have of their social world and the way it is changing. This kind of understanding is quite distinct from that usually associated with contemporary urban sociology. It is often argued, for example, that concepts of country and city give us decreasing analytical purchase on the way in which advanced capitalist societies are developing. Yet notions of country and city form a regular part of people's experience and understandings.

We have so far discussed these themes as though we were constructing a wholly new kind of urban sociology. This, however, is not the case. A central argument of this chapter is that we can gain much by rereading and reinterpreting old, now relatively unfashionable, forms of sociology. Much of this work has indeed come under increasing criticism. It will be argued here, however, that this criticism has resulted in overlooking a number of the older works' most important insights. So if we retrace our steps through the history of urban sociology we will actually find much there that we can use to construct a sociology that reflects people's understandings and the ways in which localities and locales are incorporated into these feelings.

We start this chapter by discussing some of the early sociologists, especially those concerned with one of our main themes; the impacts of widescale social change on human association. Secondly, we take a fresh look at the Chicago School of Urban Sociology. The many criticisms that have been made of this body of work will be recognised, but again we will be arguing that it has much to teach us, especially as regards incorporating an understanding of instinctive behaviour into an understanding of social relations and moral careers. But, since the days of the Chicago School, there has been a growing divergence between sociology (including urban sociology) on the one hand, and psychology and biology on the other. This leads us to a brief discussion of the developments within these fields since the time when the early sociologists were working. These developments are exciting and suggestive, but they are frequently overly deterministic. They claim, that is, that their particular kinds of explanation offer a total explanation of human behaviour. But if we do not take their most far-reaching claims too seriously, and if we attempt to combine their insights with those stemming from more conventional social science, we can develop a form of sociology which once more has the extensive scope of the early pioneering studies.

FROM AN 'OLD' TO A 'NEW' SOCIETY: A CORE SOCIOLOGICAL THEME

A central theme in the nineteenth and early twentieth century legacy of sociological theory (and one closely linked to Giddens's argument that social life is being stretched over time and space) was that society was changing from one based on a small-scale and close-knit community of primary relationships based on blood, kinship and close association. It was becoming an industrialised society constituted by highly impersonal secondary relations. This change, it was argued, threatened social cohesion. It was also seen as inflicting profound effects on individuals' lives. To adequately understand the beginnings of urban sociology we need to develop this theme a little further.

Durkheim is perhaps the key protagonist of this dominant theme of profound social change. His main concern was to understand social order and its maintenance as the older institutions of control (for example, the family and religion) were undermined. Underlying this analysis was a profound, and from our viewpoint salutary, concern with the relationships between, on the one hand, the psychological and biological bases of people's existence (what he called their 'pre-social' lives) and, on the other hand, their lives as part of human societies and collective groups. He argued that a fundamental conflict was taking place during the period of social modernisation. Durkheim saw the social order, and the moral obligations it placed on individuals, as a barrier to the realisation of their basic and instinctive drives. At the same time, he envisaged these innate and largely egoistic tendencies as threatening to the social order. The risk associated with societal modernisation was, therefore, that the individual passions would run riot. Social cohesion was thereby at risk.

Nevertheless, Durkheim saw signs of hope. The emergent divisions of labour in industrialised society were also a prime means by which modern societies were still sustaining themselves in a relatively conflict-free way. The new divisions of labour necessitated by the industrial economy were in fact obliging specialised groups of people to co-operate and work together. He nevertheless still saw a need for such divisions being accompanied by new collective and community-based institutions. If this did not take place, he argued, the result would be increasing levels of crime and suicide as pre-social or instinctive, biologically-based, behaviour increasingly reasserted itself.

Durkheim saw relations within localities as having a function in these processes, albeit a mainly facilitating one. They were a means by which 'moral density' could in fact be sustained. Durkheim put this in the following way:

The division of labor develops as there are more individuals sufficiently in contact to be able to act and react upon one another. . . . But this moral relationship can only produce its effect if the real distance between individuals has itself diminished in some way. Moral density cannot grow unless material density grows at the same time, and the latter can be used to measure the former.[2]

As Nisbet points out in his review of the 'sociological tradition', the thesis of the eclipse of an older form of community recurs throughout much of the nineteenth and early twentieth century sociological tradition.[3] A central, underlying theme was that a new social order was being ushered in; one in which relations between people were being profoundly modified. Again, these relations were widely envisaged by social scientists as becoming individualistic, self-seeking, competitive and anonymous. Furthermore, such changes were being accompanied by a decline in mutualistic support between associates and kin.

Similarly, the idea that these changes in social and personal life were being partly supplanted by alternative forms of close-knit association was also shared by a wide range of authors. We have seen this already in relation to Durkheim. Tonnies (with his account of the transition from *Gemeinschaft* to *Gesselschaft*) also argued that the emergent forms of society also continued new kinds of close-knit association. For him, trade unions were an example of attempts to create a substitute for *Gemeinschaft*; one appropriate for the new era of capitalist industrialisation.[4]

Despite these common themes, however, such changes in the relationships between the individual and society were attributed to a diverse range of causes. For Durkheim, as we have seen, the level of explanation was 'community' or broad association. For Simmel (who was also influential on the Chicago School of Sociology) the individual or small group was itself the focus of explanation. In ways rather similar to Freud he argued that individualism and group differentiation stemmed less from macro processes and largely from individuals and small groups themselves attempting to assert personal identities. For Marx and Engels, by contrast, changing relationships between individuals and society had to be rooted in the class system of society itself. Similarly, alienation, crime and upheaval had much less to do with individualistic action or even changes in community association. Rather, the underlying mechanism was class relations, class struggle and the poverty generated by capital's exploitation of wage labour.

There is one final point regarding the changing forms of association which many of these early sociologists saw as characteristic of the new social order. There are some widespread and questionable assumptions in nearly all this literature as to what societies used to be like before the advent of industrialism and capitalism. Somewhat surprisingly, for example, in the early 1890s Engels wrote of workers prior to industrial capitalism as follows:

[They] vegetated throughout a passably comfortable existence, leading a righteous and peaceful life in all piety and probity; and their material position was far better than that of their successors. They did not need to overwork; they did no more than they chose to do, and yet earned what they needed. . . .[5]

Durkheim, by contrast, maintained a considerably less rosy picture of how social life used to be. The close personal associations and relations based on respect and morality were, he argued, heavily based on a repressive social order.

With some of these sociological theories we are perhaps again witnessing the process we identified earlier with the aid of Raymond Williams. One quite helpful way of understanding social change is to construct simplified, even idealised, pictures of a past community life. We must nevertheless be cautious in assuming that the changing forms of association identified by these authors are simply products of their romanticising imaginations. In the last chapter we discussed Giddens's notion of time–space distantiation; the idea that social life and social processes are becoming increasingly stretched over both time and space. The decline of community and the rise of a society in which association was becoming in some sense secondary can also be seen as reflecting some of the profound social and spatial changes that were actually taking place in the nineteenth and early twentieth centuries.

LOCALITY, LOCALE AND MORAL CAREERS: A REASSESSMENT OF URBAN SOCIOLOGY'S ORIGINS

Key elements of what Nisbet called the 'sociological tradition' were adopted by the Chicago School of Urban Sociology of the 1920s and 1930s. Their combination of classical sociology with a number of other intellectual currents led to a range of concerns which are central to our theme; especially those of locality, locale and moral careers. There have been many criticisms of the Chicago School but this body of work still has a great deal to teach us.

Firstly, let us look at the wider influence of the Chicago School. The main theorist here is Park. Of particular interest to him were those writers who were 'concerned in different ways with human nature, individual and collective consciousness and the conditions of social order'.[6] Many of the founding fathers, including Durkheim, are mentioned in his personal papers; and Durkheim's influence, especially his concern with human nature and its relation to social or 'cultural' forces, forms a central part both of Park's analysis and of the Chicago School more generally.[7]

However, other rather separate streams of thinking also influenced the work of Park and his colleagues during the early years of this century. Two of these came from the natural world. Social Darwinism was the first. Although Darwin himself fiercely resisted such thinking, it was clearly tempting to make close analogies between the natural and the social world. Indeed, the nineteenth century English philosopher, Herbert Spencer, had already constructed theories of human society based on Darwin's evolutionary ideas and his writings were again part of Park's reading.

Park, however, was not attempting a direct and obvious analogy between the workings of nature and those of human societies. Rather, he was arguing that there is indeed a 'biotic' level to human behaviour, one constituted by instincts of survival and competition. As such, he saw Darwinian theory as having something to say to social scientists, even though he also emphasised that there is a 'cultural' level specifically associated with conceptualising human beings. But, although Park and the Chicago School recognised these two levels of human behaviour, it should be said that they did still engage in some largely unhelpful metaphors between the social and the natural worlds. A particular, and somewhat misleading, borrowing by the Chicago School from the natural world consisted of analogies with plant life. Ecology envisages a complex sorting process taking place as different types of plant compete for space. This competition takes the form of 'invasion' and 'succession'; the stronger species eventually occupying the territory occupied by the weaker. Eventually (and assuming some kind of drastic disruption does not take place) a given space tends to settle down into a state of balance. The 'beech tree climax' is an oft-quoted example of how a particularly dominant species exercises long-term domination over the natural life of a particular area.

The Chicago ecologists compared these processes with those of the social world. The prices that different social groups are able to afford for land can be seen as an equivalent to natural species competing for space. Businesses, house buyers and so forth also compete for the same space, the strongest (i.e. those who can offer the highest price) eventually gaining the most favourable positions. So a 'climax state' for the modern industrial city is one in which the central areas are dominated by powerful business interests. Meanwhile, the remaining parts of the city are occupied by those unable to offer effective competition.

The result is again a sifting out and segregation of the city into well defined and specialised areas. As Park put it:

There are forces at work within the limits of the urban community – within the limits of any natural area of human habitation, in fact – which tend to bring about an orderly and typical grouping of its population and institutions.[8]

Even within residential areas a segregation process takes place; the richest residents being those who displace the economically less powerful groups. We will discuss shortly the social significance which the Chicago urban sociologists attached to the these zones. But we must remember that, unlike social Darwinism, there was no question here of importing the theory directly into the human social world. Rather, the idea was to see people as simultaneously subject both to natural and instinctive drives while at the same time caught up in the various forms of culture and social relations which human societies construct in a more conscious way.

Park's personal papers also show other influences on the Chicago School's thinking. Sumner and Thomas were especially important. Sumner was concerned with what he called 'folkways'; people's customary acts and institutions which satisfied an individual's instinctive needs. His work foreshadowed that of Maslow and Malinowski who we will review in Chapter 7. Sumner saw hunger, love, vanity and fear as key forces underlying individual behaviour and people developed a number of social institutions to maintain these needs. Out of sex and love, for example, grows the institutions of marriage and the family. Out of fear of insecurity emerges the institution of marriage. More generally, the instinctive drive for self-preservation led to the emergence of a range of public and governmental institutions.

Individuals and their relationship to the social world were also the prime concern of Thomas. Like Sumner, he was interested in the intersection between individual behaviour and society, in particular with how social groups imposed a range of standards and mores as a result of the broad social circumstances in which they were located. Thomas was trying to combine an understanding of the biological and instinctive drives underlying individual behaviour and the society of which these individuals formed part. The starting point for him, however, was individual behaviour; people's own understandings of the world and the broader social changes flowing from such understanding. As Thomas put it: 'if men define situations as real they are real in the consequences.'[9]

Perhaps the key influence on the Chicago School was, however, G. H. Mead. As discussed in the last chapter, it was this author particularly who stressed the significance of the expressive order in understanding social processes and social relations. He was again interested in the construction of 'self' in the social world. Indeed, he proposed a two-stage process in which individuals' identities were constructed. At an early stage it is formed in relation to the child's experience, especially its relationships with other children in play. But the full realisation of 'self' comes through participation in the larger society. This latter is what Mead called the 'generalized other':

> The organized community or social group which gives to the individual his unity of self may be called the 'generalized other'. The attitude of the generalized other is the attitude of the whole community. Thus, for example, in the case of such a social group as a ball team, the team is the generalized other in so far as it enters – as an organized process or social activity – into the experience of any one of the individual members of it.[10]

The 'generalised other' Mead saw as a form of reference group; a means by which some individuals assessed their norms and values in relation to some external authority.

By implication, of course, those who chose not to become part of the 'generalized other' were less than fully developed. An unspoken assumption is that those not adopting the attitudes of the early twentieth century American 'other' were personally underdeveloped and possibly even deviant.

Language, for Mead, was the key means by which this socialisation takes place. He recognised that human society is characterised by extraordinarily complex and rich forms of communication, and it is through such communication that the individual's self is constructed and the larger group is constructed. As Mead put it:

> Language in its significant sense is that vocal gesture which tends to arouse in the individual the attitude which it arouses in others, and it is this perfecting of the self by the gesture which mediates the social activities that gives rise to the process of taking the role of the other.[11]

As mentioned previously, Mead was one of the early originators of symbolic interactionism, a perspective on social life which emphasises the significance to social change and social order of the understandings and interpretations which people hold both of themselves and of others.[12] It is this perspective which links us to the work of Goffman, Harré and Giddens. Goffman was a graduate student at Chicago in the late 1940s and early 1950s, and his concern with how people present their selves (including their 'front' and 'back' selves) in the process of conversation lies firmly within the symbolic interactionist tradition.

As we shall see shortly, many of these themes (especially the links between individual and social behaviour) formed a central part of the Chicago School's work in the field of urban sociology. There is, however, one remaining important element of their work. The Chicago School's work was overwhelmingly empirical. Park and his colleagues were strongly influenced by 'pragmatist' social science. This meant that concepts and ideas had continually to be tested against specific problems confronted in particular situations. Conceptualising, therefore, is best understood as the mental effort that people make in understanding their circumstances and attempting to find solutions to the practical problems and frustrations they find on a day-to-day basis. Furthermore, the meanings of concepts changed in the very process of everyday life and the search for solutions to problems.

The members of the Chicago School were, therefore, actively developing their theories in the process of trying to understand the problems and changes with which they were surrounded. And the surrounding transformations and tensions were indeed challenging. Between 1898 and 1930 the population of Chicago doubled, to become some three million people. Most importantly, this was almost entirely the result of immigration, first from the European countries and, following the First World War, from southern USA. The Chicago School's writings are full of facts and figures relating to what they called, using a plant ecology metaphor, the 'invasion of newcomers and the social implications of these changes'. Cressey, one of the Chicago sociologists, wrote in 1930:

In 1930 one quarter of the people were of foreign birth, and an additional 40 per cent were the children of foreign parents. Only two cities in Poland have more Poles, and but two cities in Ireland have more Irish than are to be found in Chicago. In addition Chicago is the third largest Swedish city in the world, the third largest Bohemian, the third largest Jewish, and the second largest Negro. There are seven immigrant groups in Chicago, each composed of over one hundred thousand people, in addition to which there are nearly a quarter of a million Negroes.[13]

The social significance of this (and one linking it to the theorists we have discussed earlier) lay in the fact that large numbers of individuals, uprooted from their established communities and families were adapting to one another and to the existing Chicago population. Such invasions were seen as bringing about conflict, sometimes of an extremely violent nature. Figures 2.1 and 2.2 remind us that this was also an era of sporadic, but vicious, feuds between whites and what they saw as the invading blacks. As Cressey put it:

Where the groups are of similar social and economic level with no particular dislike for each other, the supplanting of one group by another usually involves only a minimum of friction. But where marked prejudices exist and there is a fear that the invading group will cause a serious loss in real estate values, violent opposition may develop. This situation has arisen particularly in the expansion of the Negro population into white communities and has been the reason for numerous bombings and other types of violence.[14]

To put all this another way, Chicago represented for its sociologists an ideal case study area in which to test the grand theories of sociology; the changing social relations resulting from a shift from a pre-industrial to an industrial society, the effects this had on the individual and what Goffman was later to call the 'moral careers' of people as they managed (or indeed failed to manage) with the circumstances and institutions in which they were caught up. How did the Chicago School actually achieve these objectives?

MORAL CAREERS AND THE CITY: THE CHICAGO SCHOOL'S APPROACH

Note that we have not yet encountered a specifically 'urban' explanation of social change. As Saunders has convincingly demonstrated, none of sociology's founding fathers relied on the idea that cities and city life were themselves causing social transformation.[15] It was, in fact, Weber who was clearest about this. According to Weber the city's real social and political significance was limited to the particular historical circumstances of the mediaeval period. It was then a forcing ground for the new classes establishing themselves and exerting their power against the existing feudal order. As Saunders puts it:

Essentially, Weber's essay sets out to show how the mediaeval cities in Western

Figure 2.1 Black couple being escorted to a safe area during the race riot, 1919. (From H. Meyer and R. Wade, *Chicago: Growth of a metropolis*, University of Chicago Press, Chicago, 1969. Courtesy of Chicago Historical Society.)

Europe sustained a fundamental challenge to the feudal system which surrounds them, and thus paved the way for the subsequent development of a rational–legal social order. This challenge emanated partly from the erosion of traditional values and the development of new forms of individualism, and partly from the usurpation of traditional powerful landed interests and their replacement by new forms of individualism, and their replacement by new forms of domination on the part of wealthy merchants and the urban nobility (as in the 'patrician cities') or later (and especially in Italy), on the part of the entrepreneurs and artisans organised through urban guilds (as in the 'plebeian cities').[16]

Yet the Chicago School of Urban Sociology was attempting a specifically 'urban' theory of social change; one applicable to the new times of a modernising, industrialising society. They were equating (and as Saunders points out this was later to lead to confusion) Mead's concern

Figure 2.2 Whites chasing a negro during the race riot, 1919. The mob cornered him under the house in the foreground and stoned him to death. (From H. Meyer and R. Wade, *Chicago: Growth of a metropolis*, University of Chicago Press, Chicago, 1969. Courtesy of Chicago Historical Society.)

with the relations between self and society, with these relations as they were being constructed in specific *geographical* contexts such as Chicago or one of Chicago's zones. Clearly, there are real problems in equating 'society' or 'community' wholly with the limited, if very important, interactions in which people involve themselves in particular localities. So, although this perspective still has much to teach us, we shall subsequently be combining it with the broader explanations offered by later urban social theorists.

One of the most famous essays emerging from this attempt to give spatial significance to the Chicago School's broader theme of self and society was Burgess's 'The growth of the city: an introduction to a research project'. Here is its opening:

The outstanding fact of modern society is the growth of great cities. Nowhere else have the enormous changes which the machine industry has made in our social life registered themselves with such obviousness as in the cities.[17]

In other words, the Chicago School closely follows the classical sociological tradition in being centrally concerned with the transition from a pre-industrial to a post industrial society. Park was perhaps the most influential early member of this group and it was he who, in tracing this transition, distinguished between what they called the 'biotic' and 'cultural' levels of human behaviour. Cities and community structure he saw as reflecting *both* the instinctive or natural forms of individual and group behaviour *and* the various forms of conscious social behaviour. So the biotic and the cultural levels are both concerned with individual and collective behaviour. However, it was the first of these, the competition and relationships forged in the struggle for survival (including the economic struggle), which Park argued was specific to human ecology. This links to the Chicago School's borrowing from Darwin. *The Origin of Species* had shown that competition between animals and between plants led to adaptations between different breeds and the eventual dominance of some breeds over others. Similarly, these continuing contests in the natural world were leading to *areas* which were specialised in their functions. In a similar way, Park and his colleagues argued, the growing city was developing as a set of specialised yet interacting physical communities as they adapted in relation to one another. As Park wrote in *Human Communities*:

Competition operates in the human (as it does in the plant and animal) community to bring about and restore the communal equilibrium when, either by the advent of some intrusive factor from without or in the normal course of its life history, that equilibrium is disturbed.[18]

So unconscious and spontaneous forms of behaviour were of special interest to these early members of the Chicago School. It was this biotic aspect of human behaviour to which they gave special attention in trying to understand how populations and individuals adapted to one another and how this sorting process resulted in spatial distributions of social groups. They thus gave specific attention to the instinctive bases of human behaviour, this being much more than an attempt to make an analogy between the human world and the struggles for survival identified by Darwin in the natural world. It was a genuine attempt to explore the innate bases of behaviour and their social implications, even if something of the confused Darwinian metaphor remained.

Nevertheless, the Chicago School of course recognised the various forms of conscious and institutional forms of control which only conceptualising human beings could achieve. Bearing in mind later criticisms of this work (by, for example, Alihan) arguing that the Chicago sociologists never made clear which elements of social behaviour were cultural and which biotic, it is important to emphasise that, in line with Durkheim, Sumner and other earlier social theorists, Park and his colleagues continued to emphasise the close relationships between these two forms of explanation. The idea was that the distinction should not be apparent when it came to examining human activities and social relationships in actual urban areas. Park describes the particular signifi- cance of the biotic level of human behaviour to natural areas in the following way. Note, however, his parallel insistence on the cultural level.

The urban community turns out, upon closer scrutiny, to be a mosaic of minor communities, many of them strikingly different from one another, but all more or less typical. Every city has its central business district; the focal point of the whole urban complex. Every city, every great city, has its more or less exclusive residential areas or suburbs; its areas of light and of heavy industry, satellite cities, and casual labor mart, where men are recruited for rough work. . . .

These are the so-called *natural areas* of the city. They are the product of forces that are constantly at work to effect an orderly distribution of populations and functions within the urban complex. They are 'natural' because they are not planned and because the order they display is not the result of design. . . . In short, the structure of the city, as we find it, is clearly just as much the product of the struggle and efforts of its people to live and work together collectively as are its local customs, traditions, social ritual, laws, public opinion, and the prevailing moral order.[19]

Generations of schoolchildren have learnt that the Chicago School's famous concentric rings diagram (Figure 2.3) was simply a physical picture of the way in which cities expand. Yet this is of course only a very partial view of what these sociologists were attempting. Essentially, they were trying to examine the progress, or indeed lack of progress, of the immigrant newcomers as they tried to settle into this physical and social landscape. The city was envisaged, then, as a social cauldron; one in which the struggles between the old and new ways of life were being actively conducted.

The city centre, the 'zone of transition', was where the new immigrants often started their moral careers. This was the area of slum, the zone of maximum social and personal deterioration. Yet, and here Burgess partly reflects the early sociologists' emphasis on the new forms of collective organisation, this area of deterioration 'is also one of regeneration, as

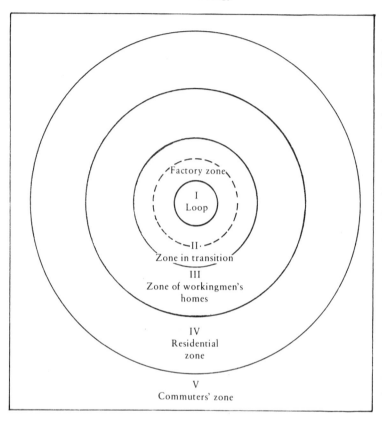

Figure 2.3 The growth of the city. (From Burgess (1925) in R. Park *et al.*, *The City* (rev. edn), University of Chicago Press, Chicago, 1967. Reproduced with permission.)

witness the mission, the settlement, the artists' colony, radical centers – all obsessed with the vision of a new and better world'.[20]

For the middle class reformers at least, this 'new and better world' was represented by the rings further out of the city (Figure 2.4). Beyond was the area of second generation immigrant settlement.

It is the region of escape from the slum, the *Deutschland* of the aspiring Ghetto family. For *Deutschland* (literally 'Germany') is the name given, half in envy, half in derision, to that region beyond the Ghetto where successful neighbors appear to be imitating German Jewish standards of living. But the inhabitant of this area in

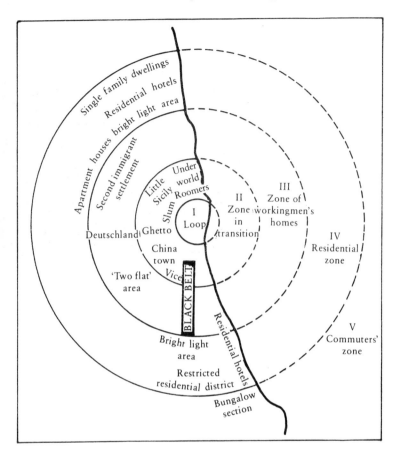

Figure 2.4 Urban areas. (From Burgess (1925) in R. Park *et al.*, *The City* (rev. edn)., University of Chicago Press, Chicago, 1967. Reproduced with permission.)

turn looks to the 'Promised Land' beyond, to its residential hotels, its apartment-house region, its 'satellite loops' and its 'bright light' areas.[21]

In short, one way of understanding Burgess is that he is describing the moral careers of immigrants; some successfully adapting and eventually living in what they and respectable Chicago society saw as the 'front regions' of the desirable suburbs. Others, however, never escape from the central, and deteriorating, areas; these perhaps envisaged as 'front regions'

for their supposedly deviant occupants but 'back regions' for the
dominant orders of American society. Social mobility, therefore, is again
closely linked to spatial mobility. We might note here the central role of
locales in these processes. The physical segregation of the city 'offers the
group, and thereby the individuals who compose the group, a place and a
role in the total organisation of city life'.[22]

The final key point about these analyses are their emphasis on broader
social change. Again, this closely parallels one of the grand themes of
early sociology we discussed earlier, the changing relation of the
individual to other members of society and the wider social implications
of this relation. Mobility, Burgess argued, has great impacts on both
individual and social life. As he put it:

The mobility of city life, with its increase in the number and intensity of
stimulations, tends inevitably to confuse and demoralize the person. For an
essential element in the mores and in personal morality is consistency, consistency
of the type that is natural in the social control of the primary group. Where
mobility is the greatest, and where in consequence primary controls break down
completely, as in the zone of deterioration in the modern city, there develop areas
of demoralization, of promiscuity and of vice.[23]

In other words, the rapid shift of populations through the zone of
transition meant that primary forms of community and social control
were collapsing. Face-to-face associations were becoming temporary,
fragmented and instrumental. For pleasure and stimulation in this zone of
transition many people turned to a criminal way of life. As we have seen,
the Chicago sociologists had every reason to be concerned with gangs
engaging in a criminal behaviour. Chicago was, of course, *the* leading
capital of organised North American crime, with rival ethnically-based
groups repeatedly engaging in open warfare.

So the elements of a spatial sociology which we discussed in Chapter 1
are actually well represented in these older forms of urban sociology. Here
we encounter, for example, locales, localities, front and back regions and
activities, moral careers, changing forms of face-to-face association and
an abiding concern with physical space in the making of individual and
collective identities. Figure 2.5 shows one way of redefining the early
Chicago School work. It shows what they saw as the moral careers of
'successful' and 'unsuccessful' immigrant and the spatial progress from
back region to front regions which is bound up with these careers. But, as
this figure also suggests, this is in fact a view which accepts dominant
(white, middle class) views as to what constitute a city's back or front

regions. An alternative view is represented by Figure 2.6. These same regions might well be viewed rather differently by gang members who (by choice or otherwise) stay in the transitional zone. This zone may well be the front zone where they attempt to gain the respect of other gang members. Similarly, a respectable suburban life may well be suppressed by an individual who wants to retain credibility amongst the gang.

Many of the early Chicago School's themes, albeit with different emphases, recur in its later work. Take, for example, the well known 1938 essay by Louis Wirth, 'Urbanism as a way of life'. He again argued that cities were themselves the cauldron in which the transition from the old to the new societies was taking place; and, crucially, cities were themselves actively generating a new way of life. Society, he said, was no longer based on small groups scattered over large territories. Rather:

The distinctive feature of man's mode of living in the modern age is his concentration into gigantic aggregations around which cluster lower centres and from which radiate the ideas and practices that we call civilization.[24]

So cities were again seen as having causal effects. Like Park, however, Wirth was not arguing that the effects of city life could be considered separately from the rise of capitalist industry. Rather, the argument was that industrialism was giving rise to new, and massive, urban concentrations and these latter were having distinct social effects. Nevertheless, like the cities of the pre-industrial era, modern industry-based urban areas were mechanisms for sustaining human contact.

The rise of cities in the modern world is undoubtedly not independent of the emergence of modern power-driven machine technology, mass production, and capitalistic enterprise; but different as the cities of the earlier epochs may have been by virtue of their development in a pre-industrial and pre-capitalistic order from the great cities of today, they were also cities.[25]

Then follows Wirth's famous definition of the city. 'For sociological purposes a city may be defined as a relatively large, dense and permanent settlement of socially heterogeneous individuals.' The point of this definition was, however, that it should be used. The central objective was to establish the kinds of actions and organisations that people typically make for themselves in this kind of social and spatial environment. He comes to a similar conclusion to that of the classical theorists of the nineteenth century: face-to-face contacts are many and multifarious, but they are again secondary, fractionalised and based on only a very partial knowledge of a particular individual. The resulting effects, as people

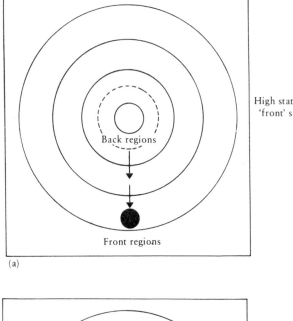

High status in moving to a
'front' surburban region

(a)

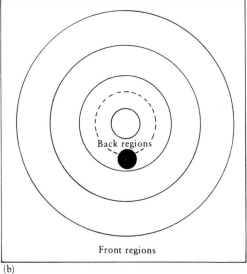

Low status in staying in a
'back' inner city region

(b)

Figure 2.5 Moral careers, spatial mobility and middle class values. (a) A
'successful' immigrant. (b) An 'unsuccessful' immigrant. (After Burgess, 1925.)

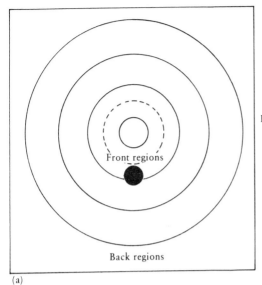

High status in staying in a
'front' inner city region

(a)

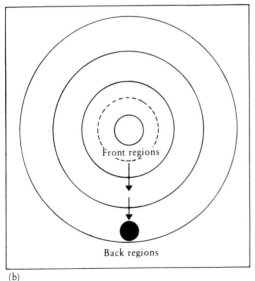

Low status in moving to a
'back' suburban region

(b)

Figure 2.6 Moral careers, spatial mobility and subcultural values. (a) A
'successful' immigrant. (b) An 'unsuccessful' immigrant. (After Burgess, 1925.)

attempt to create their own personal and insulating space (what Harré refers to as *Umwelt*) are profound:

> The reserve, the indifference and the blasé outlook which urbanites manifest in their relationships may thus be regarded as devices for immunizing themselves against the personal claims and expectations of others.[26]

So Wirth argues that a distinct kind of 'urban personality' emerges in the new city; one distinguished by competition, aggrandisement, mutual exploitation and separation from nature. Furthermore, individuals are rendered 'schizoid' by the range of roles which they undertake and which they experience in others. Similarly (and this is a point we develop in later chapters) 'there is little opportunity for the individual to obtain a conception of the whole or to survey his place in the total scheme'.[27]

In the less well known studies of particular subcultures, the Chicago School develops the theme of moral careers and the effects of space. An example is Cressey's 1932 study of the 'taxi dance hall', a commercial institution in which men purchased dances from young women.[28] For the young women, many of whom were 'set adrift in a money-mad city life', the taxi dance hall fulfilled a basic desire for social recognition. This was, nevertheless, an increasingly commercialised society and 'the impersonal attitudes of the marketplace very soon supersede the romantic impulses which normally might develop'.[29] The taxi dance hall was, therefore, a complex combination of the outright commercial exploitation of women *and* these women's search for some kind of identity.

For the women this involved a distinct moral career. The 'lowest' level was the 'overnight date'. Here the taxi dance hall represented little more than clandestine prostitution. Above this level, however, a young woman was 'faithful' to three or four men. As one of the men put it, 'two of us paid her rent, another paid her groceries and a fourth fellow bought some of her clothes'.[30] The highest status level was that of the 'mistress' – a more permanent relationship.

Other studies, such as Whyte's 'Social structure, the gang and the individual' and Thrasher's *The Gang,* combined studies of moral careers (in particular those of the Italian immigrant community) with their use of locales.[31] American society, Whyte argued, placed great emphasis on upward social mobility. The 'Cornerville' man is caught in a contradiction. On the one hand, he is tempted to advance himself materially 'through advancement in the world of rackets and politics'.[32] On the other hand, precisely by moving upwards and into his 'front region' he loses his original connections and identity.

For all the attempts to move upwards, however, there remain massive constraints and limitations. The fact of living in the back region itself leaves a social stigma. Hence he is more or less permanently associated by middle class opinion with a back region. Thus

[It] is difficult for the Cornerville man to get onto the ladder, even on the bottom rung. His district has become popularly known as a disordered and lawless community. He is an Italian, and the Italians are looked upon by upper-class people as among the least desirable of immigrant peoples.[33]

The gang, Whyte argued, had a distinct internal structure of seniority; though a structure which allows upward mobility within it. The abiding informal rules are the meeting of obligations for the rest of the gang. Those who do not meet their obligations (lending money, helping out in other ways) stand no chance of moving up the hierarchy. The leader is one who does systematically meet obligations. Furthermore, one of his main attributes is the capacity to link to other gangs and their leaders. This internal seniority structure and pattern of mobility might seem to be the sole mechanism underlying the making and breaking of gangs. But, as Whyte points out, the situation is in fact more complex than this. The actual formation of gangs depends as much on the splits and alliances made by the gang leaders as on the gangs' internal dynamics.

Finally, we can again recognise the central role of locales. *Within* a back region there are, of course, fronts and backs. In this area, the 'corner' is a front region. Cornerville man describes the gang member and his relationships in a very literal sense. As one member put it to 'Bill' Whyte:

'Fellows around here don't know what to do except with a radius of about three hundred yards. That's the truth, Bill. They come home from work, hang on the corner, go up to eat, back to the corner, up a show [sic], and they come back to hang on the corner. If they're not on the corner, it's likely the boys there will know where you can find them. Most of them stick to one corner. It's only rarely that a fellow will change his corner.'[34]

Several of these themes are present in Thrasher's remarkable study of 1,313 Chicago gangs. The overall conceptual framework is again that of the biotic 'struggle' for existence, the key result being the creation of distinct, 'natural' areas. In this instance we are again studying a very real struggle, with gangs looting, scavenging and turning to organised crime as a means of scraping together a living. Within this framework four particular themes stand out. One is the familiar picture of gang life emerging from an area of high social and spatial mobility and hence of

Figure 2.7 A detached worker meets members of the Junior Vandals and Midget Navahoes in a restaurant hangout on the Near North Side. (From F. Thrasher, *The Gang*, University of Chicago Press, Chicago, 1927. Reproduced with permission.)

isolation from dominant mores and habits. 'Demoralisation' here refers literally to the 'development of attitudes and habits which are out of adjustment with the dominant social codes'.[35] The detached individual (see Figure 2.7) thereby joins a 'criminal gang'. This gang may well have:

[its] own mores, which govern the relations of its members to each other, and it may have a high degree of morale, developed in fighting other gangs or defying the law'.[36]

A second theme is again locale; the settings in which the gangs hang out. These form what he calls 'the conditioning factors within which the gang lives, moves and has its being'.[37] These back regions are formed in what he calls the 'interstitial regions' abandoned as the city has grown out.

[Gangland is] isolated from the wider culture of the larger community by the processes of competition and conflict which have resulted in the selection of its population'.[38]

But, even within Gangland, there are front and back regions. The place to be seen is again the street corner (see Figure 2.8). It is here, in a communal context, that gang members (in this case the racist 'Little Murderers' and 'Big Murderers') put up a front to impress their own members, other gangs and respectable citizens.

Many of these same themes, including what Whyte called Cornerville man, recur in the postwar Chicago work. A good example is Suttles's *The Social Order of the Slum*.[39] This was a further study of the social and spatial organisation of part of Chicago's 'transitional zone', its divisions and its relations to the outside world. The district is called the 'Addams area' by Suttles; Jane Addams being the well known reformer who was operating Hull House in this area some fifty years earlier. On the one hand, Suttles argues, slum areas are 'culture building worlds', with ethnicity, territoriality and (once more) spatial organisation being the key means by which social and personal identities are made. On the other hand, these identities are constructed in relation (and partly in opposition) to the demands and views of respectable middle class opinion.

In some ways it is easiest to describe the neighborhood by how its residents deviate from the public standards of the wider community. . . . Seen from the inside, however, the Addams area is intricately organized according to its own standards and the residents are fairly insistent on their demands.[40]

Suttles's view of urban areas as the settings of face-to-face relations and interactions reads very like the concerns of Harré and other authors discussed in Chapter 1. Here, in line with Harré's model as represented by Figure 2.4, we find individual identity being formed in the process of collective association and interaction. The means by which these identities are formed are, according to Suttles, the withdrawal of ethnic minorities to small territories and a limited range of personal associations. Nevertheless, personal identity and worth (and hence 'moral careers') are constantly being assessed and judged in this immediate social context.

Addams area residents relate to one another primarily by personalistic morality in which individual precedent is the major standard of evaluation. The most incongruous of people become associated and continue to remain safe companions. Judgements of worth and social sanctions are individuated and tailored to past commitments. Normative rulings, then, do not apply to a fixed role apart from the incumbent; they can be developed only as individuals have the time and occasion to become familiar with each others' past history and future intentions.[41]

Many of the other themes identified earlier recur in this more recent

Figure 2.8 The 'murderers' little and big. Most Chicago gangs were divided into junior and senior divisions. The top picture shows the 'little murderers' playing Sunday morning games. Below, the 'big murderers' gather on a street corner diagonally across the street. The gang gained its name from the 1919 race riots when it killed several negroes. (From F. Thrasher, *The Gang*, University of Chicago Press, Chicago, 1927. Reproduced with permission.)

work. As suggested above, this slum area may well be the context in which 'fronts' are being put up by individuals in the processes of day-to-day interaction. But what Suttles calls the 'public view' in fact stereotypes this same area as a 'back region'. Like a prison community, it is seen by respectable opinion as an area incapable of acting in what he calls 'an approved social manner'. Moreover, the public view affects how people in the slum actually behave. Like those in the closed prison community, the stereotype is often lived up to.

In so far as the residents depend upon the public definition of each other, there is very little basis for trust except through the exercise of brute force or economic sanctions.[42]

Physical space again forms a key element in the social and personal processes of identity-formation. On the one hand, large-scale capital movements, investments and political strategies create a physical land-scape of shopping centres, streets and public buildings. But at the same time these physical forms are the means by which each group (including Negroes, Italians, Mexicans and Puerto Ricans) actively monitors, and sometimes resists, the incursions of others.

TOWARDS A REFORMULATION OF THE EXPRESSIVE ORDER

Although the Chicago School over-used the Darwinian metaphor of the struggle for survival, and although it made the mistake of equating 'society' or 'community' with the social systems of relatively small areas, the Chicago School still has much to offer in terms of the new kind of spatial sociology which we started to develop in Chapter 1. It was engaging with much the same processes as those later explored by Goffman, Harré and those working from a symbolic interactionist position. Of particular interest is the Chicago School's sensitivity to localities and locales as the context of human interaction, the formation (though moral careers) of personal and social identities and large-scale social transition forming and *formed by* small-scale interaction. In short, the slum (and other parts of the city) had their own kinds of mutually agreed social order. The question must arise, therefore, why this kind of urban sociology has become unfashionable.

The answer lies largely in the kind of critique that we developed earlier in relation to Harré. It certainly sees urban concentrations as resulting from industrialisation and capitalism: but it rapidly places these considerations to one side and looks to interactions between people as the prime explanation. Park, adopting an analogy with plant and animal ecology, was interested in how individuals adapted to the larger, and rapidly changing, society of which they were part. Wirth gave special emphasis to the social-cum-physical setting of cities as themselves giving rise to secondary and partial human association. All this gave powerful ammunition to urban sociologists writing from the mid-1970s onwards.

Castells is particularly significant here. He argued that neither of these perspectives had theoretical objects. As regards adaptation, for example, he made the critique which we made above in relation to front and back regions. Adaptation actually meant adaptation of immigrants to the norms and values of capitalist America. As he wrote:

Not only does this branch of urban sociology have a non-special theoretical object (viz. everything which takes place within an urban setting) but it has a different and non-explicit: the process of acculturation to modern society, i.e. to American society.[43]

As a Marxist (and, in his early days, structuralist Marxist attributing relatively minor significance to the actions and understandings of individuals and groups) Castells therefore found the Chicago School offering very partial understandings. And such explanations only contributed to the existing capitalist social order. Furthermore, even if acculturation to a dominant order was a feature of early Chicago society there was, according to Castells, no need to promote this as a universal process occurring in all cities. The Chicago School work, Castells argued, at best offered good empirical studies of a very specific set of historical circumstances. So, in sum, Castells's argument leads to the suggestion that people's moral careers, their use of back and front regions, and so on, cannot be considered separate from the workings of a capitalist economy or the exercising of political authority. As he wrote in 1976:

As soon as the urban context is broken down even into such crude categories as social class, age or 'interests', processes which seemed to be peculiar to particular urban areas turn out to be determined by other factors.[44]

The question, however, is whether Castells's wholesale and penetrating critique represents the end of the matter. Our argument here is that it does not. Social theory generally (and urban social theory especially) cannot afford to lose sight of people's own understandings of the social world.

To do so would seriously undermine our understanding of how people are not only constrained by, but also through their actions change, the deeper structures in which they are caught up. The concerns of the Chicago School are still relevant, even if they require supplementing by reference to social relations and processes. People's understandings, as we have earlier seen pointed out in Williams's *The Country and the City*, need placing in the wider social circumstances in which they are living. Similarly, their moral careers need placing in the context of their class position in employment, as well as in the physical and social context in which they live. Again Cornerville man or the taxi dancer are operating within capitalist, patriarchal and, frequently, racist societies.

The point here, however, is that the expressive order, moral careers and front and back regions are still constructed and lived, albeit within extraordinarily persistent social structures which constrain and enable people's lives. The implication is that the critiques developed by Castells and others have partly missed their targets. While the Chicago School certainly addressed the expressive order in problematic ways, their critics have thrown out the baby with the bathwater; misinterpreting or misunderstanding what these sociologists were attempting. The task now is to reconstruct a new kind of urban sociology which combines both kinds of insight. However, this has not taken place. Much progress has been made since the days of the Chicago School in terms of understanding the biological and instinctive bases of individual and social behaviour. Yet this progress has remained debilitated by a refusal to link such understandings with those concerning what the Chicago School would have called the 'culture' which human beings consciously make for themselves.

THE EMERGENCE OF A DIVIDED URBAN SOCIOLOGY

We have seen the Chicago School making the important distinction between the biotic and cultural levels of human behaviour, and we have seen them attempting to combine these understandings of individual and social behaviour in the study of the 'natural area'. The clinical distinction between the biotic and cultural levels is difficult to sustain and urgent attention (of the kind being developed by Harré *et al.*) needs to be given to the merging of these two lines of thought. Nevertheless, the Chicago School at least tried to relate an understanding of the instinctive aspects of human behaviour to conscious forms of individual and social behaviour, even if we remain unhappy with the precise way in which this combination was brought about.

Since the heyday of the Chicago School, though, there has developed in urban sociology (and, arguably, in sociology more generally) a major gulf between these two kinds of understanding. Throughout this study we will be discussing the crucial contributions made by recent writers within the social (or what the Chicago School called 'cultural') level. We will find, for example, Marxists giving primary emphasis to class relations, their uneven development and the shifting alliances between classes in particular localities. We will also find feminist writing, giving special emphasis to patriarchal gender relations and their different forms in employment, the neighbourhood and the home. Other authors, especially those influenced by Weber and Foucault, emphasise the role of bureaucracies, their power over subordinated populations and their control over different economic and social interests affecting domestic and community life. We return to these in Chapter 5.

These perspectives are quite familiar. So too are recent developments in what the Chicago School would have seen as the biotic level of instinctive behaviour affecting individuals and societies. Biology and psychology have, of course, developed considerably since the 1920s and 1930s, and at this stage we must outline some of their basic theses. As will rapidly become clear, however, these theories have remained largely detached from the Chicago School's cultural level. So while some understanding of these perspectives must form an essential part of social theory, one giving greater credence to people's own actions, theories and understandings, we must insist that these instinctive (biotic) processes are mediated by social (cultural) processes and relationships.

Contemporary understandings of the biotic order: Ethology and sociobiology

The mediation of instinctive processes by social ones is largely absent from most of the recent work on the instinctive bases of individual and social behaviour. The linked subjects of ethology and sociobiology are cases in point.

Ethology is the study of species with particular emphasis on their interactions with the surrounding natural environment. Ethologists have followed Darwin in their prime concern with the evolution of species and the various forms of physical and behavioural adaptation that they have developed in the process of competing for survival. Species develop, it is argued, specific forms of innate behaviours and drives which are geared towards survival and reproduction and, while much of this work has been carried out on non-human species, it has indeed been applied directly to the human animal: Desmond Morris's 'naked ape'.

There are differences between human ethologists. One of the authors who addresses himself directly to our main concerns is Ardrey. His book, *The Territorial Imperative*, argues that human beings share with animals an instinctive territoriality, his argument being that this instinct lies deep in human nature and originally stems from animals' need to establish their patch. The need for a well defined area (one established through various forms of marker such as the song used by birds) is seen by Ardrey as having its basis in guaranteeing access to food and space for breeding for future generations.[45] Territorial instincts in people may well now be disconnected from the fact that, say, food is provided on an increasingly international basis. But this does not stop people, as human animals, having evolved with deeply held and genetically transmitted territorial instincts. Ardrey, however, spoils his case by making very extreme claims for instinctive territoriality amongst humans. Wars between nations, he suggests, are wholly a product of people's territorial natures. Ardrey may well have a point here, but there is no way we can afford to leave out the social and political (or 'cultural') relations and processes underlying such conflicts. Not the least of these are imperialism and vested interests in the extraordinarily profitable armaments industry.

More subtle and sophisticated writers in the contemporary ethological mould are Tiger and Fox.[46] The fundamental argument is again that human beings are still very 'basic' beings; that is, they have evolved over millions of years and that what we call civilisation or culture represents only a fraction of human history. As a result, we are still designed around extremely basic forms of behaviour; forms geared towards individual and social survival, despite the fact that people now live in societies where the such behaviour is largely redundant for simple survival. As Tiger and Fox put it:

We have to make the imaginative and unsettling leap into understanding that *agricultural and industrial civilizations have put nothing into the basic wiring of the human animal*. We are wired for hunting – for the emotions, the excitements,

the curiosities, the regularities, the fears and the social relationships that were
needed to survive in the hunting way of life.[47] [my emphasis]

Human beings are therefore seen as having a seventy million year old
'wiring'. Tiger and Fox argue, however (and here they part company with
the early sociobiologists), that human beings' wiring is capped by a
symbolising, conceptualising brain. This brain itself, however, is a form
of adaptation which has allowed human beings to become the dominant
species. Selection has favoured those organisms which have scientific,
learning, rule-obeying capacities all of which contribute towards the
development and maintenance of advanced societies. Nevertheless, the
'wiring' is constructed in such a way as to ensure that certain kinds of
social relationship and hierarchy processes remain reproduced.

Tiger and Fox argue, for example, that there is a special bond between
mothers and children, essentially based on suckling. The home thereby
acquires a special significance; an institution protected by the males, if
necessary by aggressive actions towards others. On the other hand,
institutions such as the family and marriage are not seen as innate or
wired. 'They are' in Tiger and Fox's words 'devices to protect the
mother/child unit from the potential fragility of the mating bond'.[48]
Another key set of wired bonds is that between adult males. While
females are reproducing and suckling, males remain programmed to hunt
and to defend their patch against predators. Linked to this is Tiger and
Fox's third main bond, that between adolescent males. Here, in the
process of competition and play, juveniles are establishing the skills
required in male adulthood. These not only include the aggression
originally necessary for survival. Adolescents are also learning how to be
loyal to the group and, if necessary, to sacrifice their own selfish ends to
those of the group. A special kind of morality, therefore, emerges
amongst male adolescents, one again originally programmed to serve the
overarching imperative for survival.

Sociobiology also envisages long-term evolution and adaptations of
animals (including human beings) as essentially organised around the
reproduction and expansion of animal and human life.[49] For
sociobiology, however, the central mechanism involved in such reproduction and expansion is not the species or even the individual but what
Dawkins calls the 'selfish gene'.

Genes and their behaviour are the basic building blocks for this
understanding of human social life. The expansion, or attempted
expansion, of genes is seen as the central causal mechanism underlying

both individual and social behaviour. Genetic reproduction and expansion has, of course, been for millions of years the basis of animal life and its evolutionary change. Needless to add, these processes (and, more arguably, the forms of behaviour to which they give rise) have a far longer history than any particular society or mode of production.

Sociobiology's central idea is that an organism such as an animal or human being acts and competes for resources in such a way as to maximise its reproductive success. This basically refers to success in spreading genes to later populations; even if this means damage to an individual organism's success. At its simplest, sociobiology is arguing, then, that the central drive affecting individual and social behaviour is not the preservation of the individual but the maximisation of the individual's genes into future generations. This behaviour goes beyond simple biological reproduction. It includes innate male aggression and, as recognised by some ethologists, an emphasis on instinctive territoriality.

Sociobiology therefore extends its field of analysis well beyond the individual organism. It incorporates the concept of 'inclusive fitness'; the sum of an individual's fitness plus that of other blood relatives. This principle of inclusive fitness is perhaps summed up by the answer reportedly given by the distinguished biologist J. B. S. Haldane when asked in a bar whether he would lay down his life for his brother. His reply, after an extended pause, was 'not for one brother. But I would for two brothers or eight cousins'.[50]

So the emphasis in much contemporary biology is now shifting away from the earlier Darwinian concerns which, as we have seen, originally influenced the Chicago School. If the earlier understandings were based on individuals, species and their 'fitness' for survival, the present concern is with behaviour stemming from shared genes. Individual animals and people are seen as people or animals acting as 'survival machines', being largely programmed by their genes towards the expansion of inclusive fitness and the use of resources to that end. And these resources include, of course, other organisms.

Thus organisms are seen primarily as means by which strands of DNA are reproduced through succeeding generations. Sociobiology develops from this an understanding of instinctive social and individual behaviours which stem from these innate drives towards maximising reproductive success. For any one such machine, the environment within which he or she is competing includes not only the natural environment in the form of air, light, water and food, but also other survival machines. These, too, are seen as programmed to act in the reproductive interests of their genes.

These machines compete and evolve so that those which survive are those which have best adapted to their genes' demand for replication and expansion.

Competition for scarce resources is seen by sociobiology as involving various forms of behaviour. Competition and struggle may be the watchwords but this does not necessarily imply outright hostility. If competition generated raw aggression resulting in defeat or death this can hardly be seen as assisting fitness maximisation. The picture painted by sociobiology is less one of outright and explicit aggression and more one in which individuals or species evolve what Maynard Smith calls 'evolutionary stable strategies'. These are learned and inherited forms of individual and social behaviour which, assuming no major upheaval in the environment takes place, tend to be best for reproductive success.[51]

The maximisation of reproductive success is seen by this perspective, as socially based. That is, an individual's selfish genes are envisaged by sociobiology as leading to a number of self-preserving strategies which are essentially collective in nature. Inclusive fitness is the key concept here; with altruism, more than individual selfishness, being a form of behaviour most likely to guarantee reproductive success.

Altruism here refers to the various forms of self-sacrifice, or, more accurately, apparent self-sacrifice, in which animals and human beings engage. However, as Haldane's comment suggests, altruism is seen as a function of the proportion of genes shared by individuals. A person or animal inherits half its genes from each parent. For two siblings there is a fifty-fifty chance that it will share one of its genes. This means that if one sibling helps another to survive and reproduce then it is ensuring the further spread of its genes within future generations. To a decreasing extent, the same principle can be seen as applying to other blood relations. Kin altruism is therefore seen by sociobiologists as the most basic form of co-operative behaviour. It refers in particular to the forms of sacrifice which parents make for their children to expand their genes into the 'gene pool' of the population as a whole.

Kin altruism is not, however, seen as the only form of altruistic behaviour in which sociobiology sees people and animals engaging. 'Reciprocal altruism' is envisaged as the second main form of social behaviour. Essentially this refers to forms of altruism between unrelated individuals. While altruism by one individual towards another clearly involves some self-sacrifice, the tacit (even unconscious) assumption by the donor is that such sacrifice will, in the long run, generate reciprocal support. The underlying motive here (although the word 'motive' is misleading since it suggests that such strategies are not genetically driven but are a product of conscious strategy) is again 'the selfish gene' and its reproductive success.

The third main form of social behaviour introduced by sociobiology is 'induced altruism'. This is a process whereby altruistic behaviour by one individual remains uncompensated. Meanwhile, the recipient of this altruism stands a better chance of survival and, more importantly, its genes stand improved possibilities for replication and expansion. The classic form of induced altruism in the animal world is, of course, the bird raising the cuckoo's egg. But as Badcock and others argue, the same principles can be applied to all forms of human and animal life.

Whenever one organism promotes the fitness of another at its own expense and without reciprocal benefit to itself or benefit to its own genes present in the recipient it has perforce performed an act of induced altruism.[52]

There are, however, a number of difficulties with this perspective, and especially about the core issue with which we have been concerned. How is an understanding of biological processes to be applied to the social world? One involving, for example, relationships between classes or between men and women as they are socially constructed?

There is firstly, however, the question of whether the sociobiological arguments are correct even on their own terms. There is now (as we have seen Tiger and Fox recognising) a wealth of anthropological data on the evolution of man as a conceptualising, language-using animal. Recent research by Leakey and Lewin in Africa shows that the most characteristic feature of early human beings is their large brains.[53] This suggests, Leakey and Lewin argue, considerable conceptualising capacities: consciously relating to others through language and reflecting on the innate processes to which they are subject. In short, the characteristic feature of human beings, as the early symbolic interactionists such as Mead emphasised long ago, is that they are *self-aware* in a sense in which other animals are not. This means that there is a specifically human nature to the early *homo erectus* which Leakey and Lewin reckon was roaming around East Africa 1½ million years ago. He and she had capacities for self-awareness, reflection and organisation through a well organised and complex language. Self-awareness means that human beings are, in fact, capable of engaging pure altruism. This does not imply that there are no innate drives, including inner biological drives, nor that human beings are always likely to act in a selfless way towards others. It does mean, however, that we must consider human beings as conceptualising animals, reflecting on what is taking place to them and, furthermore, doing something about it. It is precisely through the evolution of conceptualising capacities (and, in particular, of language enabling complex social interactions) that human beings have come to dominate other species.

The second, and related, argument against sociobiology is that sociobiology is engaging in biological determinism; the central accusation being that it offers a wholly biological basis for social and individual behaviour. Sahlins has pressed this argument particularly hard, criticising what he calls 'vulgar sociology' which suggests 'a one-to-one parallel between the character of human biological propensities and the properties of human social systems'.[54] For a radical social theorist such as Sahlins (and for a number of feminists) sociobiology is no more than a means of justifying the status quo as inevitable and 'natural'. To quote Sahlins again:

What is inscribed in the theory of sociobiology is the entrenched ideology of Western society: the assurance of its naturalness, and the claim of its inevitability. Since the seventeenth century we seem to have been caught up in this vicious cycle, alternatively applying the model of capitalist society to the animal kingdom, then reapplying this bourgeoisified animal kingdom to the interpretation of society.[55]

Sahlins's criticism of sociobiology centres on his analysis of human kinship in contemporary pre-industrial societies. He argues that each form of kinship has its distinctive form of arrangements. In some societies, for example, distantly related individuals may be incorporated into the formally recognised family, while in other cultures even children may be excluded. He argues, in short, that actual forms of kinship are socially constructed. None of them actually obey the formal theory which suggests that altruism towards kin in human societies is directly in proportion to shared genes.

Sahlins's arguments have strength. Indeed, they are much in line with the argument we have been developing. On the other hand, he is in danger of slipping into a wholly cultural (and Marxist) determinism. Furthermore, he is actually criticising an early, and distinctly primitive, form of sociobiology. More recently, anthropologists and others sensitive to this kind of criticism and conducting empirical research from this perspective have become much less assertive and deterministic. So while the expectation of altruism mathematically relating to kin relatedness is almost inevitably doomed to be disproved in human societies, there is now considerable evidence that sociobiology identifies some broad relationships and tendencies which are incontrovertible. Kin relations are a particularly good example. Betzig, on the basis of a survey of a wide range of surveys, writes that:

More has been written about whether or not people take kinship into account when they expend reproductive effort than about any other problem in the study of human reproductive behaviour. People have been shown (1) to prefer proximity to kin (presumably, the better to help them), (2) to actually help their kin (presumably in ways likely to enhance their reproductive success), and (3) to produce more children and grandchildren when they live close to and/or are helped by kin.[56]

Despite such increasing subtlety, however, this new approach to what the Chicago School would have called the biotic level remains relatively asocial. While there may well be an overall tendency for people to support kin, there are considerable class differences in the extent of this mutalism. Dunbar, amongst current researchers operating from a broadly Darwinian perspective, offers salutary (and, for ardent sociobiologists, perhaps the most disheartening) advice:

In my view, those who concentrate on a search for species-wide universals in behaviour or morphological traits are likely to be disappointed. The number of genuinely universal traits are, I suspect, likely to run to single figures at most and probably correspond to the handful of biological 'needs' like warmth, food and procreation. Beyond that, everything else is essentially a context-specific attempt to put those few universal principles into practice.[57]

Clearly, any attempt to understand the instinctive or biotic bases of human behaviour is fraught with immense complexities and difficulties. Furthermore, any attempt to promote the biological and instinctive bases of human behaviour at the expense of social relations and processes is surely doomed to failure. A large part of our difficulty stems from the dualism between man and nature which was established in Western philosophy well before the establishment of modern science and sociology.

One answer, and a point we will develop at the end of this book, is to recognise that ethology and biology may well have identified some of the most basic relationships and processes (preservation of self and kin, territoriality, different forms of bonding between parents and children, male aggression) underlying human behaviour. As such, sociology (including urban sociology) may well have been premature in rejecting these kinds of understanding. There is no logical reason to reject the idea that sociological concerns (with, for example, class, power and gender) are not based on biological and deep-rooted psychological foundations.

We return to some of these links in later chapters, but might note here, for example, the extent to which ethology comes round full circle to reach conclusions very similar to contemporary radical feminist analysis. Ethology's assertion that male aggression has an instinctive basis to it has a close parallel with those radical feminists such as Dworkin who argue that males are inherently and innately violent.[58] Despite long-held opposition by many feminists to sociobiology and ethology (the most common basis to the feminist argument being that male aggression is entirely culturally derived) their conclusions are very similar. But the possibility of radical feminism recognising biological and instinctive bases of male violence is spoilt by the early ethologists and sociobiologists overstating their case. A recognition of these instinctive processes and relations does not of course entail envisaging all social behaviour as an unmediated result of underlying primordial processes. Rather, some combination of instincts and social processes is taking place.

What the sociobiologists have identified are some underlying relationships and *latent* forms of human behaviour. But whether, how, where and when these underlying instincts are activated is a social (or what the biologists would call a 'cultural') matter. Furthermore, these forms of behaviour are not simply direct responses to external stimuli. People, of course, have the capacity to give their own meanings to their and other people's actions.

Freud and his discontents

The other main element of the biotic sphere of human and social life which would be built into our new kind of spatial social theory is social psychology. Although the Chicago School made passing reference to Freud's work in discussing the biotic level, it did not explore it in detail, perhaps because it was not fully available in English during the 1920s and 1930s.

Social psychology is clearly another large and highly complex topic. As with the discussion of ethology and sociobiology, however, we shall simply be considering some of the main themes in this area (especially those deriving from Freud) and their possible links to the biological work we have just discussed. We can also make some preliminary connections to some of the issues with which 'urban' sociology is conventionally concerned.

Again, these links must not be rushed at; social psychology cannot be 'read off' into urban sociology in the way in which some authors have attempted. Firstly, there are also (as with biology) some internal inconsistencies to social psychology which need making clear. Secondly (and there are again close parallels with sociobiology), there is the outstanding problem of social psychology's apparent 'asociality'. How, in short, are we supposed to relate this kind of work to what the Chicago School called the 'cultural' sphere of consciously constructed relationships and structures? As we discuss shortly, this particular problem has also been explored in depth by feminist writing.

There is clearly a strong argument for social theory (including 'urban' social theory) being thoroughly involved in these knotty problems. On the other hand, this literature is not easily applicable to the 'urban' sphere or even to the 'social' sphere more generally. Arguably, Jung's psychology (one which appears to link better to collective experience and social relations) is in some respects a departure for a new sociology which is more sensitive to the relationship between the individual and society and to 'moral careers'. As shown in Chapter 1, it is indeed this type of psychology which Harré *et al.* select as most appropriate for the 'new psychology' which they are constructing.

Freud, however, is a more common starting point for social theory. There are a number of connected themes here. Initially, at least, two particular sets of ideas seem most directly relevant to conventional 'urban' concerns.

First, there is the difficult question of ownership. Does the possession of such items as domestic property and land have an instinctive basis?[59] Freud's psychoanalytic theory argued that people are innately possessive. This stems, he said, from a child's early toilet training. Very young infants are loathe to give up their precious bodily products and this is largely because children gain pleasurable sensations from not doing so. Later child psychologists have noted how older children find and hang on to a favoured object such as a rag. This is the beginnings of property acquisition, stemming from the need to be secure in relation to the outside world. We shall shortly assess the plausibility of this notion.

Secondly is Freud's understanding of the human personality's different levels. For him the 'id' represents basic, primordial drives and sexual instincts. The 'superego', however, is a censoring, evaluating, mechanism, one instilled into children at an early age. It is thereby often based on a childhood authority figure such as the father or mother. Such a figure tends to replicate itself in the relationships and practices in which children engage in later life. The 'ego' (itself linked and responsive to the id and the superego) is constantly searching for what Freud and later Freudians call 'defence mechanisms' to protect and enhance individual personality.

This links to our 'urban' concerns through considering Freud's ideas of how social groups come into being (including, for example, those formed on a neighbourhood or local political basis). In his later works, Freud was particularly interested in the psychology of social and political groups.[60] He argued that the leaders of such groups, and the altruistic ideals which they appeared to espouse, had a deep psychological significance for the other members of the group. Children, having built up in the early stages of their lives an 'ego ideal' with whom they have had apparently satisfactory relationships, are for the rest of their lives attempting to transfer this ideal on to other people or organisations. Classically, of course, this may well be a sexual partner. But, beyond this, an individual's identification with this idealised figure (usually, but not always, a parent) is transferred to other individuals or organisations. Meanwhile, of course, apparently satisfactory early relations with a mother or father may well, according to Freud, have been based on the repression of sexual urges.

Freud extended his analysis of close-knit sexual and blood relations to the formation of larger social and political groups. He argued that many organisations (especially those that were relatively long-lasting and dependent on leaderships for their organisation and continuance) could be interpreted in terms of the transference of early childhood affections. Individuals' 'ego ideals' are seen as being systematically transferred to charismatic leader figures, organisations and the values (including those of family, church and patriarchal authority) which are no less than a displaced version of the all-providing 'father' or 'mother' figure of childhood. As Freud wrote:

A primary group of this kind is a number of individuals who have put one and the same object in the place of their ego ideal and have consequently identified themselves with one another in their ego.[61]

Freud had always supposed that the various forms of innate behaviour he explored had biological bases to them. These connections continue to be explored by psychologists who have studied the relationships between evolutionary genetics and the subconscious.[62] If the id represents basic primordial drives, it can be argued that this is a psychological equivalent of the biological tendency towards fitness maximisation in human beings. Similarly, as Badcock argues, the ego can be seen as a means by which tactics for maximum fitness are constructed by active, conscious, social human beings. The ego's tactics towards fitness-maximisation can therefore be envisaged as conditioning primordial drives in line with external circumstances and a sense of self-identity or personal defence. Finally, the superego again acts as regulator over the tendency towards maximum inclusive fitness. The displaced or externalised mother or father figure (including, of course, the state) can be seen as a repository of tradition and culture, again regulating people's innate drives towards survival and genetic representation in later generations.

Like sociobiology, these speculations and connections regarding what the Chicago School would have termed the 'biotic sphere' are exciting and provocative. Moreover, it is tempting to translate them directly into human social and political affairs. Smith is one author who makes such a translation. He argues that Freud's later work is in fact directly applicable to 'urban' social theory. 'When Freud spoke of civilization', Smith writes, 'he had in mind the process of "modernization" and the characteristics of urban life in the industrial capitalist cities of his own time'.[63] So Smith is arguing that Freud's analyses were conducted at a time when society was still undergoing a fundamental shift towards not only an industrialised society but one characterised by the growth of large cities. Freud, as Smith points out, saw the new kinds of collective social controls as suppressing basic natural desires, and, as a result, these instincts were being channelled into other more harmful forms such as aggression. Smith summarises Freud in the following way:

On the one hand, the customary inhibitions and externally imposed social controls characterizing modern urban life dilute the intensity of individual pleasure derived from the gratification of deep-seated instinctual impulses. Tamed instincts may protect the individual from vulnerability to external aggression or from emotional abandonment by one to whom he or she is fully committed in an act of love; but in the process they also render life experiences flat and stand in the way of necessary instinctual release.[64]

There are, however, a number of difficulties with this. First is the elision of newly industrialised with 'urban' societies. Freud may have been writing at a time of increasing urbanisation resulting from rapid industrialisation, but it is not at all clear that his work has any specifically 'urban' connotations. Unlike the Chicago School, for example, he was not attempting to construct an understanding of how distinct forms of 'natural area' were resulting from people's search for identity. Perhaps more important, and there are close parallels here to our critique of ethology and sociobiology, Freud still skirts round the difficult question of how primordial instincts are socially constructed. The 'individual' in the extract above is confronted by social controls. But he or she still seems to be unencumbered by, for example, the class, gender or ethnic relations which are of course socially constructed. As we shall see, this is a point which has been made most forcefully by recent feminist writing.

One way of approaching the non-cultural (or non-social) aspects of psychological theory is to start with what seems at first sight like a simple series of internal inconsistencies in Freud's work. Giddens in particular has pointed to the very varying ways in which Freud used the words id, ego and superego.[65] Sometimes, for example, the id refers to a section of the mind, at other times it appears to be alluding to a whole person or agent. As Giddens points out:

Freud writes, for example, of the ego's 'wish to sleep', although while asleep it 'stays on duty' to protect against the worst emanations of the unconscious, 'guarding' the sleep of the dreamer. . . . Whose sleep is it the ego desires? The agent's? Its own?[66]

Giddens argues that these 'terminological inconsistencies and transitions seem to indicate here some rather more significant conceptual troubles'. This leads him to put forward an alternative, three-point scheme for understanding the individual's conscious and subconscious behaviour and its relation to the social world. This scheme consists of the 'basic security system', 'practical consciousness' and 'discursive consciousness'. The first refers to the 'ontological security' which we discuss in Chapter 1: the attempts by people to gain some understanding and a sense of 'self' and social identity in the natural and social worlds. 'Practical consciousness' refers to the knowledge of the social world incorporated into actors, but, a knowledge which they cannot directly express through speech. 'Discursive consciousness', by contrast, refers to 'what actors are able to say, or to give verbal expression to, about social conditions, including especially the conditions of their own action'.[67]

As is clear from the above, Giddens's querying of Freud is more than a pedantic concentration on sloppy terminology. Giddens is trying to incorporate an understanding of the individual and his or her search for 'ontological security' with an understanding of the social world. As such, this perspective again links to the discussion of ontological security and 'escape attempts' in Chapter 1. Giddens achieves this by locating an understanding of the human agent (and the drive for ontological security) in the context of social structures and social processes. These latter, he insists, do not exist outside human action. Social structures are simultaneously resources and constraints affecting people's actions. At the same time, however, they are also are product of these actions.

Giddens again, therefore, approaches the question of locale in a more indirect but more convincing way than those who have attempted to apply psychology directly to 'urban' or 'spatial' processes. Modifying

Freud's understanding of the human agent means first that he is trying to understand the attempt of human beings to place some order on to the natural and social world under conditions of 'time–space distantiation'. Once this point is reached, we can then start gaining a more useful understanding of the social and personal significance of people's instinctive notions of the 'urban' and the 'rural'. As Williams argues, these are ciphers or lay theories representing ways of life and contexts for apparent self-determination.

Giddens is not the first, however, to suggest that Freudian ideas are insufficiently 'social'. The problem has, in fact, been extensively argued during recent years. Take first the question of property. The tendency amongst many contemporary psychologists is to give less significance than Freud to the purely psychosexual aspects of property.[68] The argument would now tend to be that a child refusing to be toilet trained is not simply enjoying the experience for its own sake. He or she is actually trying to exercise power over nurse or mother. Similarly, older children's possessive impulse would now not be seen as an instinct for ownership *per se*. Rather, their attempts to maintain exclusive rights over an object are seen as attempts to create their 'selves' and their relationships to other groups of children. In short, if there are indeed innate or instinctive psychological mechanisms which are passed on genetically, then these take distinct social forms. Trasler summarises his survey of the recent literature on the psychology of property in the following way:

It is not possible to explain the vast structure of institutions to which we assign the name of *property* as the expression, the means of satisfaction, of man's desire for physical objects. Even the earliest possessions, as we have seen, have meanings for the individual which are social, that have to do with his relationship with others and his standing among his fellows.[69]

A parallel argument is put by contemporary feminist writers when they discuss Freud's ideas regarding relationships between parents and children. Starkly put, did Freud establish some of the great universals of personal being and family relations? Or was he simply placing a cloak of scientific respectability over the peculiarly oppressive relationships of turn-of-the century Vienna? The second argument is put forcefully by Firestone when she argues that the sexual repression Freud describes and the adoption of parent (especially father) figures by children which they carry through into later life can only be seen in the social context of oppressive patriarchal relations in the home. Freud, though initially shocking to respectable middle class opinion, replaced an emergent feminism. As Firestone puts it: 'Freudianism subsumed the place of feminism as the lesser of two evils'.[70] For Firestone the alternative is to supplant Freudianism (and, by extension, psychotherapy) with an explicit acknowledgement of socially constructed and reproduced power; especially power of men over women and power of parents over children.

   This, however, is not the end of the argument. Mitchell is amongst those who argue against Firestone and hold out for the continuing relevance of Freud's work. She suggests that Freud was fully aware of the extent of patriarchal power. 'What he was interested in was how this social reality was reflected in mental life'.[71] Furthermore, she argues that Freud would not have shared Firestone's confidence about an objective social reality to which mental life must adapt. In short, she argues, radical feminism is accusing Freud of not doing something which he never set out to do. In the process, it manages to ease out mental and biological life altogether, once more subsuming it as a wholly social construct. Mitchell therefore insists on relations between men, women and children having an instinctive as well as a purely social basis. She achieves this by attributing to Freud a relatively low level of transhistorical applicability. It is therefore Mitchell's study which best fits the general argument being developed here.

COMBINING THE BIOTIC AND SOCIAL ORDERS

This chapter first reviewed older forms of sociology, including the Chicago School of Urban Sociology. This work contained a number of problems, not the least of which was their equating society and locality, and their clinical and unproblematic distinction between the biotic and cultural orders. On the other hand, they were far more sensitive than we now are to the instinctive or innate bases of human social behaviour. This led us to identify a number of key themes in the contemporary literature concerning what the Chicago School called the biotic order. Clearly, much of this literature from the natural sciences remains contentious; the counter-arguments largely stemming from ethological, biological and psychological theory's avoidance of the social world. Nevertheless, this literature must be taken much more seriously by social theory generally, as well as by urban social theory.

   A number of important, and highly linked, themes emerged during our discussion of the contemporary literature on the biotic order. These included innate self-preservation and support for kin and generations; aggressive tendencies from juvenile males; affiliatic individuals with groups and displaced parent figures; innate drives ownership or exclusive access; the search for ontological security anc especially significant for us, instinctive territoriality.

If these are instincts which human beings have inherited over several million years, any understanding clearly entails demonstrating how they are combined with the social and cultural relations of contemporary society. Few contemporary social scientists recognise this. Timpanaro is an exception. He chastises Marxists for asserting an economic and social determinism at the expense of considering that people actually are born, reproduce others and eventually die. As he puts it:

To maintain that, since the 'biological' is always presented to us as mediated by the 'social', the 'biological' is nothing and the 'social' is everything, would once again be idealist sophistry.[72]

Similarly, Hirst and Woolley have challenged not only biological and psychological reductionism, but the idea that conventional sociology also has a monopoly of wisdom:

Sociologists have, on the whole, energetically denied the importance of genetic, physical and individual psychological factors in human social life. In doing so they have reinforced and theorised a traditional Western cultural opposition between nature and culture.[73]

CONCLUSION: URBAN SOCIOLOGY, A CORE TENSION

The above critiques are easy enough to make but the more difficult question is what to do about them. At this point we can usefully remind ourselves of the central problem with which urban sociology is engaged and the reasons why we are engaging in the problematic areas of theory discussed in this chapter and in Chapter 1.

In the Introduction and in Chapter 1 I rehearsed Giddens's argument concerning 'time–space distantiation' in contemporary societies and resulting ontological insecurity. Social life is increasingly centralised and concentrated; national and multinational organisations and governments having increasingly dramatic impacts on people's lives. At the same time, most people's daily lives and face-to-face contacts remain relatively limited to small-scale localities. Indeed, the recent decline in spatial mobility means that daily life is increasingly limited to relatively small regions. This tension between locally-based life and nationally or internationally based markets and governments leads to what Giddens calls 'ontological insecurity', a condition in which people have a limited understanding and control over their circumstances and the processes affecting their daily lives. Such insecurity leads to 'escape attempts' or local utopias in which a degree of autonomy and identity can be secured.

This tension explains why we are addressing the biotic and expressive orders. The first, as discussed in Chapter 2, refers to the relatively unconscious struggle for survival and the establishment of personal identity. The second, as we saw in Chapter 1, refers to people's understanding of the world; this understanding leading to social action and communication. An understanding of the biotic and expressive orders supplies us with an improved appreciation of human agency; one which means we need no longer envisage people as automatic pilots swept along by the broad forces of capitalist processes and social relations. The biotic and expressive orders help explain why people suffer from ontological insecurity, and why (and how) they attempt to create zones of relative autonomy.

In reviewing the literature in both these areas we have encountered a recurring theme. This is that the work of such authors as Harré, Goffman, Freud and Ardrey remain insufficiently 'social'. The social order has gone largely missing. This is ironical since it is in this sphere that urban sociology, and arguably sociology more generally, has made its greatest recent advances.

The following chapters have two main purposes. Firstly they discuss how a consideration of the expressive and biotic orders can be linked to the social order and applied to the fields of study currently examined by more conventional urban sociology. But secondly, and more assertively, they examine the extremely diverse ways in which ontological insecurity is both generated and overcome. As discussed in the Introduction, the actual extent of such insecurity and the extent to which 'escape attempts' are successful varies according to the particular sphere of social life with which we are concerned. As social life becomes increasingly organised at a global level, the sphere of employment perhaps offers least prospect for the assertion of autonomy and personal identity. By contrast, the sphere of civil society offers greater prospects for self-determination. The gains to be made in the political sphere are, as Chapter 5 will show, more ambiguous and contradictory.

NOTES AND REFERENCES

1. R. Harré (1979) *Social Being,* Blackwell, Oxford, p. 312.
2. E. Durkheim (1933) *The Division of Labour in Society,* Free Press, New York, p. 262.
3. R. Nisbet (1966) *The Sociological Tradition,* Heinemann, London.
4. F. Tonnies (1955) *Community and Association,* Routledge, London.
5. 'Want leaves the working man the choice between starving slowly, killing himself speedily, or taking what he needs where he finds it – in plain English, stealing. And there is no cause for surprise what most of them prefer to starvation and suicide.' F. Engels (1969) *The Condition of the Working Class in England,* Panther, London. p. 30.
6. D. Smith (1988) *The Chicago School,* Macmillan, London, p. 120.
7. It is worth noting here the considerable influence of the Chicago School of North American Sociology as a whole. See Smith, op. cit.
8. R. Park (1957) *Human Communities,* Free Press, New York, p.1.
9. Thomas is quoted in *International Encyclopaedia of the Social Sciences,* Macmillan, New York, 1968.
10. G. H. Mead (1934) *Mind, Self and Society,* Chicago University Press, Chicago, p. 154.
11. G. H. Mead (1934) op. cit., p. 160–1.
12. For introductions to the symbolic interactionist position see for an example H. Blumer (1969) *Symbolic Interactionism,* Prentice Hall, Englewood Cliffs, NJ; and J. Manis and B. Meltzer (eds) (1980) *Symbolic Interaction,* Allyn & Bacon, Boston. For an illustration of how symbolic interactionism can be combined with reference group theory and class analysis and how such a combination can be used to examine social change in specific localities see in particular J. Urry (1973) *Reference Groups and the Theory of Revolution,* Routledge & Kegan Paul, London.
13. P. Cressey (1971) 'Population succession in Chicago, 1898–1930', in J. Short (ed.), *The Social Fabric of the Metropolis,* Chicago University Press, Chicago, p. 111.
14. P. Cressey (1971) op. cit., p. 113.
15. See chapter 2 of P. Saunders (1986) *Social Theory and the Urban Question,* Hutchinson, London.
16. P. Saunders (1986) op. cit., p. 35.
17. E. Burgess (1967) 'The growth of the city', in R. Park and E. Burgess, *The City,* Chicago University Press, Chicago.
18. R. Park (1957) op. cit., p. 47.
19. R. Park (1957) ibid., p. 196.
20. E. Burgess (1967) op. cit., p. 56.
21. E. Burgess (1967) ibid., p. 56.

22. E. Burgess (1967) ibid., p. 56.
23. E. Burgess (1967) ibid., p. 59.
24. L. Wirth (1938) 'Urbanism as a way of life', *American Journal of Sociology,* 44: 1–24.
25. L. Wirth (1938) ibid., p. 66.
26. L. Wirth (1938) ibid., p. 71.
27. L. Wirth (1938) ibid., p. 76.
28. P. Cressey (1971) 'The taxi-dance hall as a social world', in J. Short (ed.), *The Social Fabric of the Metropolis,* Chicago University Press, Chicago.
29. P. Cressey (1971) ibid., p. 200.
30. P. Cressey (1971) ibid., p. 206.
31. W. Whyte (1971) 'Social structure, the gang and the individual', in J. Short (ed.), op. cit.; F. Thrasher (1927) *The Gang,* Chicago University Press, Chicago.
32. W. Whyte (1971) ibid., p. 232.
33. W. Whyte (1971) ibid., pp. 231–2.
34. W. Whyte (1971) ibid., p. 215.
35. F. Thrasher (1927) op. cit., p. 258.
36. F. Thrasher (1927) ibid., p. 258.
37. F. Thrasher (1927) ibid., p. 106.
38. F. Thrasher (1927) ibid., p. 20.
39. G. Suttles (1968) *The Social Order of the Slum,* Chicago University Press, Chicago.
40. G. Suttles (1968) ibid., p. 3.
41. G. Suttles (1968) ibid., p. 229.
42. G. Suttles (1968) ibid., p. 27.
43. M. Castells (1976) 'Is there an urban sociology?', in C. Pickvance (ed.), *Urban Sociology,* Tavistock, London.
44. M. Castells (1976) ibid., p. 40.
45. A. Ardrey (1967) *The Territorial Imperative,* Collins, London.
46. L. Tiger and R. Fox (1972) *The Imperial Animal,* Secker & Warburg, London.
47. L. Tiger and R. Fox (1972) ibid., p. 22.
48. L. Tiger and R. Fox (1972) ibid., p. 71.
49. See, for example, D. Barash (1977) *Sociobiology and Behaviour,* Elsevier, Amsterdam; R. Dawkins (1976) *The Selfish Gene,* Oxford University Press, Oxford; E. O. Wilson (1975) *Sociobiology: The New Synthesis,* Harvard University Press, Cambridge, Mass.
50. J. B. S. Haldane is quoted in J. and M. Gribbins (1988) *The One Per Cent Advantage,* Blackwell, Oxford, p. 116.
51. J. Maynard Smith (1982) *Evolution and the Theory of Games,* Cambridge University Press, Cambridge.
52. C. Badcock (1986) *The Problem of Altruism,* Blackwell, Oxford, p. 121.

53. R. Leakey and R. Lewin (1978) *People of the Lake*, Avon Discus, New York.
54. M. Sahlins (1972) *The Use and Abuse of Biology*, Tavistock, London, p. 5.
55. M. Sahlins (1972) ibid., p. 101.
56. L. Betzig (1988) *Human Reproductive Behaviour*, Cambridge University Press, Cambridge.
57. R. Dunbar (1988) 'Darwinizing man: a commentary', in L. Betzig, op. cit.
58. See, for example, A. Dworkin (1981) *Pornography. Men Possessing Women*, Women's Press, London.
59. On this matter see G. Trasler (1982) 'The psychology of ownership and possessiveness', in P. Hollowell (ed.), *Property and Social Relations*, Heinemann, London.
60. See, for example, S. Freud (1985) *Civilization, Society and Religion*, Vol. 12 of Penguin Freud Library, Harmondsworth.
61. S. Freud (1985) ibid., p. 147.
62. See, for example, C. Badcock (1986) *The Problem of Altruism*, Blackwell, Oxford.
63. M. Smith (1980) *The City and Social Theory*, Blackwell, Oxford, p. 50.
64. M. Smith (1980) ibid., pp. 65–6.
65. A. Giddens (1984) *The Constitution of Society*, Polity, Oxford, especially Chapter 2.
66. A. Giddens (1984) ibid., p. 42.
67. A. Giddens (1984) ibid., p. 374.
68. See G. Trasler (1982) op. cit.
69. G. Trasler (1982) op. cit., p. 46.
70. S. Firestone (1979) *The Dialectic of Sex*, Women's Press, London.
71. J. Mitchell (1975) *Psychoanalysis and Feminism*, Pelican, Harmondsworth. See also K. Soper (1979) 'Marxism, materialism and biology', in J. Mepham and D. Ruben (eds), *Issues in Marxist Philosophy*, Vol. II, Harvester Wheatsheaf, Hemel Hempstead. Soper argues, unlike many feminists, that specifically female and male forms of consciousness exist and that these are often overlooked by critical social science. She does not, however, suggest that there may be genetic mechanisms underlying such differences.
72. S. Timpanaro (1980) *On Materialism*, Verso, London.
73. P. Hirst and P. Woolley (1982) *Social Relations and Human Attributes*, Tavistock, London.

3

CLASSES, LOCALITIES AND MORAL CAREERS

In the preceding two chapters we have been developing ways in which questions of locale and locality can be systematically introduced into social theory. This work makes systematic the fact that localities and locales are the context in which human interactions and conversations take place. As such they literally situate social change despite the fact that such change is increasingly the product of centralised authority and power. We have advanced 'moral careers' as another useful concept, this giving us a special purchase on that elusive quality: human agency. Moral careers, as we have seen, are lives organised around exemplary biographies. They concern the rise and fall of people's reputations, whether in the eyes of others or of the individual concerned.

In Chapters 1 and 2 we argue, however, that while the sociologies of the Chicago School, Goffman and Harré are all highly suggestive, they also tend to overlook some of the deeper social structures and processes in which individuals and small groups of people are necessarily caught up. Localities, locales and human interaction may help us to situate society and social change. They also help us to rectify the neglect of processes and emotions internal to individual human beings. But, as Giddens insists, human interactions and emotions are also constrained and constructed by social relations which are only partly related to the spatial contexts in which they take place.

The time has come to start using these concepts and arguments in relation to present-day urban sociology. The currently dominant paradigm throughout urban and regional sociology gives prime emphasis to class relations and processes. Now, while class-based relations and processes are clearly a necessary and crucial part of any understanding of the relationships between the 'spatial' and the 'social' at the urban and regional scales, these combine in a number of complex ways with other relations such as those of gender and ethnicity. Furthermore, as we discuss in Chapter 2, there are processes innate to human beings (including sexual and emotional drives) which also combine in many complex ways with 'social' or 'man-made' processes.

Let us first, however, review some of the main themes of established class-based relations in urban and regional studies and establish how they might be improved by our new perspective. Our central argument here will be that existing work fails adequately to consider people as active human beings. People are not mere units of labour. They have the capacity to think and act for themselves and, within the constraints of employment opportunities, make themselves socially and spatially mobile. Social and spatial mobility offers a crucial connecting link to our special focus on moral careers and 'front' and 'back' regions.

LOCALITY AND THE RELATIONS OF PRODUCTION

The circuit of capital (Figure 3.1) is of central significance to this area of urban sociology. Money (M) buys the commodities of labour power (LP) and the means of production (MP). It then sets in train a labour process in the realm of production (P). This creates further commodities (C′) incorporating the additional value added in the production process. These in turn are converted into money, some of which is profit (m′), some of which (M′) is put back into the circuit of capital.

There are three closely interlocking themes in contemporary urban and regional analysis which takes these class relations, and processes stemming from these relations, as their fundamental starting point. Firstly, the circuit above is used as the prime explanatory device. But, beyond this, production or employment itself is frequently given special explanatory weight. Figure 3.1 clearly shows production processes and relations as intimately linked with the circulation of capital and the consumption of commodities. But it is the realm of production itself (of paid employment) which is seen by this perspective as lying at the heart of capitalism and uneven development. As such it is this realm which is seen as eventually dominating forms of social and personal life and the progress (or otherwise) of localities.

Examples of such an approach to the sociology of urban and regional development are the work of Frobel *et al.* and Massey.[1] Frobel *et al.* argue

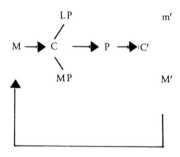

Figure 3.1 The circuit of capital.

that capital is now breaking up or 'decomposing' production processes. The result is a polarising workforce of highly skilled and qualified jobs on the one hand and deskilled, comparatively low paid, production jobs on the other. Importantly, speedier and more sophisticated forms of transport and electronic communications make it increasingly possible for these two forms of work to be in contact despite their physical separation or 'stretching' over time and space. The attraction of so-called Third World labour is the fact that it can be cheap compared to that in the advanced capitalist countries. Many of these workers may be farm workers released by mechanisation of agriculture. Industrial capital removes them from the land and subsistence agriculture.

Massey, in her work on 'spatial divisions of labour' in the British case, offers a similar conceptual framework. Again, new divisions within the labour process are seen as a crucial explanatory starting point. Upper level managers need no longer be geographically close to production processes. This means that in certain regions of advanced capitalist societies (such as, in the British case, parts of Scotland, the North East, South Wales) are becoming pools of cheap labour and lower level management, while other regions (London and the South East in Britain) have a disproportionately high number of senior managers or 'service class' personnel.

These new spatial divisions of labour have recently been further highlighted by the very rapid growth of 'services' employment. Employment in industrial production has itself declined in Britain and many other advanced countries during the postwar years. In its place has emerged a growing number of people in such work as banking, finance, insurance, property and advertising. Much of this work may well, of course, be servicing industry – in the advanced countries as well as in the developing countries.[2] The point here is, however, that these represent further rapidly growing sectors which can quite easily be spatially separate from industrial production. So Massey sees relations and changes in the realm of employment as key starting points for understanding uneven development. Unlike many writers in this tradition, however, she is especially sensitive to the effects of these large-scale processes on local social systems and on the role of labour itself effecting social change.

Another version of the 'dominance of production' argument comes from Harvey.[3] He also starts his analysis of urban and regional development with the realm of production, although he emphasises crises in the realm of production as the most important generator of spatial change. Essentially, he argues that capitalist societies are prone to periodic fluctuations in profitability. From time to time, more goods are produced than can profitably be sold and, as a result, capital must look for other forms of investment. One such is the realm of land development and property. These are 'secondary' circuits in which capital invests as a means (albeit temporary) of restoring profitability when the primary circuit of industrial capital is in trouble. The result is a series of social and physical landscapes where capital invests. But no sooner have such landscapes been created than they are destroyed before they are abandoned and neglected as capital moves off to find greener, still more profitable, pastures. The particular attraction is again cheap and disorganised labour.

The mobility of capital, not labour

Of crucial importance to these perspectives is the idea that labour is relatively passive and inactive. Implicit in both Harvey's analysis and that of most urban sociology working from a political economy perspective is the insistence that capital is globally mobile while labour is inert. In so far as people do move, they move wholly in response to capital's demand; in so far as they are active, they tend to be seen as part of a huge block of 'labour'. The central mechanism underlying spatial change is, nevertheless, capital. Capital invests where prospects for accumulation seem relatively promising (where, for example, labour is relatively inexpensive) and disinvests from areas and regions where prospects for profitability are less promising.

For Frobel *et al.*, for example, capital has been both 'pulled' and 'pushed'. It is seen as pulled not only by the reserves of cheap ex-agricultural labour in Third World countries but by the ready availability of large amounts of unskilled, young, frequently female labour for unskilled tasks. The 'push' took the form of organised, trade unionised, labour forces in the European countries. Since Frobel *et al.* were writing, however, there has emerged an argument that capital is actually increasingly finding itself drawn back to the European countries.[4] High levels of unemployment during the 1980s, for example, mean that labour forces in the older industrialised societies are not necessarily so expensive relative to those of the Third World.

So, with the exception of some authors such as Massey, the dominant paradigm to employment-related urban and regional sociology gives precious little attention to labour as an active force. Labour is typically characterised as simply waiting to be either exploited or abandoned by capital. People are pawns or units to whom things happen. The result is that little attention is given to people's own experience and under-standings of these processes and the fact that such understandings in turn lead to ways in which they attempt to improve their circumstances within the constraints and opportunities with which they are faced. No attention is given to the history of people themselves, to what we would call 'moral careers'.

People as 'class fractions'

With people envisaged as mere 'class fractions', some quite wishful thinking ensues over the prospects for mass proletarian upheaval. Industrial workers' best chance of improving their prospects is to act as a global working class. The globally-based divisions of labour produced by capital offer the prospects of mass alliance by labour against capital. For Frobel *et al.*, for example, the new international division of labour represents an opportunity for new forms of working class organisation.

A working class, disciplined for industrial work, is in the process of formation at the new sites: the organisation of these workers inside the labour process, on the production line, also embraces the possibility of their developing forms of political and social self-organisation with which they can struggle for their own development.[5]

The dominant paradigm within class-based urban and regional analysis nevertheless usually recognises the difficulties involved in creating a well-organised international working class. Perhaps the main problem for these Marxist writers is the aristocracy of labour in the advanced industrial countries. It seems unlikely that they will jeopardise their superior circumstances by combining in an alliance with Third World workers against capital. For all this, however, Frobel *et al.* remain optimistic.

The effects of the international division of labour should make it easier for workers in these countries to discard their role of real or supposed world labour aristocracy and recognise that their fate on the world labour market is inseparably linked with that of their fellow workers in the underdeveloped countries.[6]

A similar analysis comes from Harvey, although the class alliances are here seen as being at national or regional levels.[7] Geographically and socially static populations combined with the mobility of capital result in which he sees as 'factions' of classes combining with each other in an attempt to attract capital to their locality. So essentially antagonistic class interests sharing the same region find themselves allying with each other in their mutual self-interests. Even so, such alliances are, in the long run, doomed to failure. They are doomed by exploitative capital operating on a global scale.

Different factions of capital and labour have different stakes within a territory depending upon the nature of the assets they control and the privileges they command. Some are more easily drawn into a regional class alliance than others. Land and property owners, developers and builders, those who hold the mortgage debt, and state functionaries have most to gain. Those sectors of production which cannot easily move (by virtue of the fixed capital they employ or other spatial constraints) will tend to support an alliance and be tempted or forced to buy local labour peace and skills through compromises over wages and work conditions. Factions of labour that have through struggle or out of scarcity managed to create islands of privilege within a sea of exploitation will also just as surely rally to the cause of the alliance to preserve their gains. If a local compromise between capital and labour is helpful to both accumulation and the standard of living of labour (which it can be for a time), then most factions of the bourgeoisie and the working classes may support it.[8]

Exceptions to prove the rule

I have been suggesting here that contemporary class-based analyses of urban and regional development have a number of common themes.

People are largely seen as victims. Their lives, actions and politics are dominated by the demands of capital. Not all Marxists, of course, share precisely the same perspective. Warren, for example, is something of an exception to those discussed above.[9] He places, for example, much less emphasis than most Marxists on the mobility of capital, arguing that Third World countries are actually characterised by highly dynamic economies internal to the societies in question.

The reality of this picture of vibrant, 'grass roots' capitalist development in the Third World is attested to by the abundant evidence of rapidly rising commercialisation and the resulting social differentiation (especially in the rural areas of Asia and Africa), coupled with the relative expansion of wage-labour at the expense of family and self-employment, including feudal-type tenurial relationships.[10]

However, even this view of relatively autonomous, locally based development shares some of the same themes as those identified above. Class-based production processes and forces are still seen as the principal key for a useful understanding. His 'fundamental starting point' is that:

[The] development of Marxist and working-class strategy must be [founded upon] the recognition that *in general* a progressive position is one that advances the development of the productive forces.[11]

Furthermore, the working class is envisaged as just that; units (albeit divided units) of labour power. Their long-term destiny lies in united working class action and the rejection of other forms of understanding.

As Third World capitalism develops, the working class is destined to play its classic revolutionary role. The sooner this is recognised, and all forms of nationalism and populism rejected, the more successful will be the struggle for socialism.[12]

There are two closely connected points to make at this stage about these Marxist accounts. Despite their differences, their implications for the sociology of urban and regional development are rather similar. They are making the broadly accurate point that capital and capitalist social relations must form a central part of any understanding of any locality's progress. Furthermore, most of these authors (with the exception of Warren and other authors emphasising the dynamics of internal economies) argue that localities are peculiarly vulnerable to globally based movements of capital.[13]

The first, and rather obvious, point of criticism is that by concentrating on capital–labour relations and movements of capital these authors have largely neglected other kinds of relations (such as those of gender and race) which have dynamics which are relatively separate from those of class but which nevertheless combine with those of class in highly complex ways. No doubt these authors would argue that they are well aware of this problem. They would probably say that they have chosen an aspect of social life which is clearly central to many people's lives and which dominates these other kinds of relationships.

The problem is whether such a simplifying assumption does in fact adequately recognise these connections. We must insist that sociological analysis at all scales explores how these relations combine with one another. And the central point about localities is that they provide the context in which these combinations of social processes take place and in which people act as a result of such combinations. Locality studies cannot, therefore, afford to insist on simplifying and monocausal assumptions such as those often made by Marxist analysis. They must remain alive; to combinations of causes and how these combinations affect people's consciousness and actions. This brings us back to the expressive order.

Perhaps even more importantly, few of these authors in fact attempt to understand the implications of the expressive order; how the classes and class-based processes which they emphasise are appreciated or acted on by the people concerned. People understand their own and other people's lives not *just* in terms of class fractions or units of labour power even if they can be categorised as such. They may be such fractions and units but they are much more besides. Underlying their actions and understandings are, as we suggested in Chapter 1, relations which are not adequately captured by most Marxist commentators. Furthermore, since social change is constituted partly by active individuals, such understandings must have major implications in terms of understanding social change.

Very recently, however, there have emerged important signs of a change within those working within a political economy perspective. These signs, it must be said, largely reflect the changing strategies and priorities of management itself in coming to recognise that people have their personal plans and needs. Such changing managerial attitudes have been largely a result of declining profitability and the increasing challenge of Japanese firms.

Morgan and Sayer are an example of the new style of analysis within a broadly political economy perspective.[14] They point out, for example, that Japanese companies in particular have for some time been making strenuous efforts to recruit labour which is not so much cheap but flexible and prepared to work hard for the company in question. Such companies, and to a lesser extent their Western competitors, are now treating workers not as units of labour power but as people with distinct personal and social needs. Thus pay is tailored to individual performance. Recruitment procedures focus on individual skills and potential for flexible working. Company sick pay, canteens shared with managers and regular company-provided medical check-ups are all part of an attempt to make workers identify with their company.

In short, people are being treated as individuals with priorities and resources. These, the new style of management recognises, are all worth tending to. Contented workers are more likely to be profitable. The significance of all this as regards locality is that management has clear views about the regions in which these special kinds of worker are to be found. In the South Wales case, for example, there is a zone called the 'golden triangle' which is widely perceived as especially attuned to the specifications of the new, 'high tec', mainly Japanese industries. By contrast, community spirit in the valleys which were once associated with mining is seen as a threat to smooth, harmonious and profitable working conditions. To add to such an image, the local development agency responsible for attracting industry does its best to erase the old 'radical' image of the area.

Mobility and moral careers: A means of linking human agency to social structures

So political economy approaches, in line with changing managerial strategies, are now recognising the personal needs and instincts of categories of individual workers. However, the academic literature still has some way to go. Perhaps the key way to establish a connection between the concerns of conventional Marxist urban and regional sociology and the concepts outlined in Chapters 1 and 2 is to concentrate on typical forms of social mobility; the ways in which they relate to spatial mobility and moral careers. We should recall here how alive the Chicago School was to this link, even if they saw people's careers and mobility as largely products of their own actions rather than also the products of companies and other institutions. At the core of the Chicago School's analysis were the moves of immigrants from European societies to American cities and, once established in a town such as Chicago, the successful households progressing from the inner urban areas to the suburbs.

By contrast, the issue of social mobility has been almost entirely ignored by contemporary spatial analysis, even if the issue of social mobility has been one of sociology's concerns. As far as urban sociology goes, however, spatial and social mobility is what Savage calls the 'missing link'.[15]

Three points need to be remembered when we start to incorporate questions of social and spatial mobility. First is the considerable change in the class structures of advanced industrial countries. Upward mobility has been a real possibility for a large number of people. This refers mainly, of course, to the fairly well-off (and ill-defined) 'middle class'. We can be more precise than this by referring to Goldthorpe *et al.*'s work.[16] They show in the British case, for example, that under a third of the male 'service class' (people in senior management, professional and administrative positions) actually started their working lives in this class. Rapid recruitment into this class is largely inevitable as a result of a growing demand for this type of worker by the rapidly growing service sectors of the economy. But, once established, the service class is extremely effective in ensuring that its offspring also joins this elite.

The second point concerns the diverse ways in which workers, and middle class white collar workers in particular, now achieve social mobility. Some of these ways entail high *spatial* mobility and others do not. The older and best known way is as an 'organisation man'.[17] 'His' life (these people are still mainly male) and that of his family are largely dominated by the large company in which he spends most of his working life. High levels of spatial mobility are involved as he is regularly posted to regions where the multinational is operating. Often these regions may be in other nations.

The 'organisation man' picture is largely that referred to by the novelists we reviewed in Chapter 1. In fact this picture may be overworked. The second, and growing, way in which social mobility is achieved by the middle classes, and by senior white collar people in particular, is not as 'organisation men' but as workers moving quite rapidly *between* organisations.[18] For these people individualism is increasingly the order of the day. This means that many of these people do not envisage spending the whole of their working life climbing the internal labour ladder of a single organisation. Increasingly, the tendency is to work for a large number of companies in rapid succession. Alternatively, they may well work on their own account, perhaps for a number of organisations simultaneously. The result is that their high social mobility does not entail high levels of long distance spatial mobility. Rather, it involves moves *within* those regions (such as the South East) which, as described by Massey, have exceptionally high concentrations of senior white collar jobs.

This brings us to our third point, that of geographical mobility as it affects different social groups. There has in fact been a recent tendency for this type of mobility to decrease in most of the advanced industrial societies.[19] However, there remain major differences in levels of spatial mobility for different social groups. Spatial mobility tends to be highest amongst the most affluent groups on the one hand and the most poor on the other. As regards the latter, some of the most mobile in the British case are workers in personal services; those, for example, seeking work in the catering trades. A group which has received particular attention recently are the unskilled labourers moving from small-scale, mainly agricultural, work on the peripheries of the industrial economies to the economically successful regions. For capital, an alternative to migrating to cheap labour areas is to attract cheap, relatively disposable, migrant labour.

Cohen has drawn attention to this phenomenon at an international level.[20] And, for the European case, Mandel was amongst the first to demonstrate the importance of the guest workers to European capital.[21] He argues that:

Without this exodus of labour from Southern Europe, which allowed it to reconstruct a reserve army at home, West German capitalism would have been unable to achieve its formidable expansion of outputs in the 1960s without a catastrophic decline in the rate of profit. The same is true, *mutatis mutandis*, of France, Switzerland and the Benelux countries, which in the 1958–71 period together absorbed another 2,000,000 foreign workers into their proletariat.[22]

Taking, firstly, class-based urban and regional sociology on its own terms, social and spatial mobility is a major deficiency. But, assuming we do incorporate such considerations, the tendency is to interpret such mobility as again largely the result of capital's needs, with workers being uprooted simply to increase their monetary rewards, and capital benefiting as a result. This is clearly part of the story, but there is another, perhaps more subtle, way of understanding such mobility. And it is this that connects to our specific concerns with the instinctive bases of human behaviour. People's life-courses are simultaneously the product of economic structures and of people's own attempts to improve their circumstances and social standing. To illustrate this theme, we can explore some existing literature on the experience of agricultural workers on the peripheries of successful economies. Here we can see how the concepts discussed in Chapters 1 and 2 might be extended into contemporary urban and regional sociology.

We should note in passing, however, that there are a small number of studies focusing on the expressive order of the workplace which can again be interpreted with the concepts we have outlined earlier. Moral careers, escape attempts and front and back regions. These are not strictly part of our 'urban' concerns, but they do show how Harré's and Goffman's ideas, as well as Giddens's concept of 'locale' are not limited to a particular scale. Burawoy describes, for example, industrial workers' 'escape attempts'. These are informal, shopfloor cultures, industrial 'games' organised under the pressures of increased productivity. Within these cultures workers are assessing one another and their capacity to reach informally agreed levels of production.[23]

Giddens uses another illustration drawn from the car industry. One worker recalls the following episode.

I was working on one side of the car and the boot lid dropped. It just grazed the head of the fella working opposite me. I can see it now. He stopped working, had a look round to see if anyone was watching – I was pretending not to look at him – and then he held his head. He'd had enough like. He staggered, and I could see him thinking 'I'm getting out of this for a bit'. He staggered, and I could see him looking around. You know what it was like in there. Paint everywhere. He wasn't going to fall in the paint. . . . So he staggered about ten yards and fell down with a moan on some pallets. It was bloody funny. One of the lads saw him there and stopped the line. The supervisor came chasing across. 'Start the line, start the line . . .' He started the line and we had to work. We were working one short as well.[24]

Studies such as these show that the workplace, although it may present relatively few opportunities for 'escape' is also a context within which personal identity and social esteem are formed. Note that the above car worker ensures that his 'escape' from surveillance is not observed by his co-workers. Such observation would risk losing prestige. Note too how he turns a 'front' region (one subject to scrutiny from authority) into a 'back' region.[25] The more general implications of this are treated in the discussion of 'panopticism' in Chapter 5.

Returning now to the urban scale, we can illustrate our approach first with Davis's study of a small town in Southern Italy. Secondly, we can turn to Berger and Mohr's account of migrants' experience as they travel from an economically peripheral society to a thriving industrial economy in Western Europe.

Illustration 1: Social relations and moral careers in a 'peripheral' locality

Pisticci is a small town in Southern Italy still largely based on agricultural employment. When studied by Davis in the mid-1960s it was undergoing a transition from a relatively self-contained peasant society to one forming part of a much wider market economy.[26] Davis is an anthropologist, and, accordingly, his analyses are based on living with people and understanding the locality through close observation and conversations with the indigenous population.

All the themes that we have been arguing should be part of our new form of urban sociology are present in this study. The core social mechanism binding the locality together is 'honour', or what we have earlier termed 'esteem'. As Davis puts it, 'the neighbourhood, the country territory and the political network are linked by honour'.[27] Honour is a means of classifying and understanding people. It informs the whole of local social life including, in particular, people's performance in their family role. Honour is, Davis argues, 'the basis of association, of forming alliances for all purposes – mutual aid, politics, marriage, farming – from the day-to-day to the long-term.'[28] In short, people's face-to-face confrontations are primarily about 'moral careers'.

Reputation, in individuals' eyes, and in those of the surrounding locality, is therefore the prime issue of everyday life and conversation. But, as Davis is careful to point out, behind this issue are social and economic structures on the one hand and the support of kin or blood relations on the other. As regards the former, land is the great resource in Pisticci. Clearly, it is the basis of the local economy but at the same time it is the key component in marriage settlements. Land has both an economic function and a function in terms of personal and social esteem:

It is still an important component of marriage settlements, and it is an element of prestige: it can give independence of employers and it is a security for a man attempting upward social mobility. Transactions in land, particularly transactions in the exceedingly small, economically useless plots of land, are transactions in prestige and social position.[29]

Furthermore, understanding the acquisition of honour solely through a class analysis of Pisticci would miss the many subtleties engaged in by the residents. In particular, it would divert attention from the central significance of other relations such as those of kin. Using the word 'politics' in a broad sense to refer to power relations, Davis argues that:

A full understanding of the politics of Pisticci, and of communities like it, requires us to understand the idioms of kinship, friendship and clientship – as well as those of organisational rank and of class.[30]

The ways in which honour is formed and assessed are numerous. Reputation can be inherited. It can also be achieved through managing behaviour towards blood and kin. As regards a man, for example:

His behaviour towards his family is the guide to his probable behaviour in the less closely controlled and supervised political and economic spheres where, since competition is so acute, most actions appear conspiratorial, and all plans are schemes. The simple fact that he has a family at all, is a married man with adult status, is a guarantee of some element of responsibility.[31]

Marriage, therefore, brings economic and social success. It also gives to women a special status. It means that she is freed from the 'tutelage' of her father and brothers. Marriage gives her domestic independence in the form of access to the other women of the neighbourhood. And, since this network acts as the main means of managing and assessing social esteem, marriage is the main means by which women gain this form of local power.

Esteem is gained by both man and woman partly through home life, and especially through presenting 'a front space used for display', wholly distinct from a back room for sleeping and intimacy.[32] It is established too in the 'front regions' represented by the town's two small piazzas. Here public life and 'fronts' are maintained, quite separate and distinct from the secluded 'back' regions where the population lives.

How do these codes and values relate to our specific set of concerns with work and employment? Work, paradoxically enough for many small landowners and peasants, is actually an 'escape attempt', a means of being independent from large-scale farms and other industrial enterprises. But secondly, it is once more a means by which prestige and honour can be maintained. Indeed, work is one of the key bases on which honour is established in the eyes of family, kin and locality. As one Pisticci peasant puts it: 'if it were not for my family, I'd not be wearing myself out'.[33] As Davis points out, it is also a way in which wives can be saved from what is seen as dishonourable employment.

The ability of a husband to support his wife and children is as important a component of his honour as his control of his wife's sexuality.[34]

It can, of course, be argued that the great emphasis on esteem and moral careers which might be observed in a relatively undeveloped town in Southern Italy are not especially relevant to modern industrialised societies. As Davis points out, however, the increasing penetration of nationally and internationally-based market relations into this old form of society does not dispense with the overriding priority for the acquisition of personal and social esteem. Rather, it means that honour is becoming assessed in different ways. To an increasing extent, moral careers are formed on the basis of wealth and on 'impersonal economic grounds' rather than on 'moral qualities'. The old and new ways of assessing individuals exist, in fact, in parallel.

Illustration 2: Industrialisation, moral careers and the move from a peripheral to a central region

Many of the themes discussed in Chapters 1 and 2 recur in this illustration. This is Berger and Mohr's study of migrants travelling from Turkey and other peripheral regions to the more affluent regions of Europe.[35] We will encounter here Williams's emphasis on the city as a 'front' region: a romantic place representing a better life over the horizon is common. But we will encounter, too, the grim reality of the same city being an alien and sometimes hostile society with 'back' as well as 'front' regions. To maintain their own self-esteem, long-distance migrants are nevertheless obliged to repeat the myth of urban success when they return to the society they have left.

In our terms, this book is an account of migrants' moral careers, albeit careers constrained by the demands of a thriving capitalist economy. Indeed, one of the key points about Berger and Mohr's study is that such moral careers are being partly constructed by capital's requirements for a cheap workforce and one which can be dismissed in line with fluctuating demands for the products they make.

Conversations between agricultural workers on the edge of subsistence constantly refer to the city: a city that exists nowhere but which continually transmits promises'.[36] Indeed, their everyday life constantly brings about reminders of the metropolitan life. The machinery they use, their cars, their clothes, the tourists they encounter, the music they hear, all summon up the idea of a new, modern, 'front' region: one which can only be fully appreciated by actually moving and becoming part of it. Even more important than encounters with the city's products, are conversations with the people who have encountered this better life.

Those who have left and succeeded in the city and come back are heroes. He has talked with them. They take him aside as though inviting him into their conspiracy. They hint that there are secrets which can only be divulged and discussed with those who have also been there. . . .

What is not a secret at all are the wages, the things to be bought, the amount that can be saved, the variety of cars, the ways women dress, what there is to eat and drink, the hours worked, the arguments won. . . .

He recognises that they are boasting when they talk. But he accords them the right to boast, for they have returned with money and presents which are proof of their achievement. Some drive back in their own cars.[37]

Humiliating medical and literacy tests are carried out in recruitment centres. Four out of five applicants then leave their families for the supposedly better world, hoping that they will return remittances and that their kin may perhaps be able to join them later.

Inevitably, the actual experience is far removed from the dream. They are accommodated in inhospitable and humiliating barracks, well hidden as 'back' regions within this supposedly front region of a thriving capitalist economy. The work they do is itself carried out in dangerous and dingy back regions. Their jobs are those that workers in the host country refuse to do, and trade unionism is denied to them. Furthermore, the host society treats them as outcasts threatening the existing social order. The language barrier means that real interaction with the indigenous population is largely out of the question. The immigrants' behaviour is caricatured as inevitably outrageous and disrespectful. The overall result is explicit racism.

All of them carry knives. No woman is safe.
They live in those barracks like animals.
They certainly do business among themselves.[38]

Migrants are widely termed Zigeuner (gypsy), Lumpenpack (rag-pack), Kameltreiber (camel rider), Zitronen-schuttler (lemon squeezer), or Schlangenfresser (snake eater).

Outwardly he accepts this. Inwardly he calls upon his pride to remind himself who he is and what he has already achieved. The greatest of his achievements is that he is working here.[39]

The result is that they are thrown back on their own individual and collective resources. Their sexuality is largely denied. Their native music and language is, however, a means of restoring some identity and self-respect. These help them to recollect their homeland and the families they have left behind. Like the immigrants to Chicago in the 1920s, they collect in certain areas such as the local railway station to share news and experience (Figure 3.2).

Despite all these humiliations and the failure of the dream, the migrants, once they return home, find they have acquired considerable prestige.

The villagers now respect him as a man of different experience. (Given this prestige, it would be unseemly for him to take on a menial local job.) He has seen and received and achieved things which they have not . . .[40]

And to make the whole experience worthwhile to his own esteem, the returning migrant has to repeat the myth.

Is it very large, the city? His younger cousin asks him.
It is very large and to reach it takes three days and nights.[41]
Does everybody have a car?
The cars are so close together in the street that it's like a river. A river of many colours. The cars are the colours of all the fruits of the world.[42]

SUMMARY: POLITICAL ECONOMY AND MORAL CAREERS

The objective has been to indicate the value of appreciating the expressive order: the understandings people have of their own lives, their attempts to maintain self-esteem and the respect of others in the context of processes and decisions far removed from their understanding or influence. Political economy and class perspectives on urban sociology lend little credence to this type of analysis. They tend to see people as unthinking dupes who are simply pushed and pulled around by the needs of capital. Clearly, the

Figure 3.2 Yugoslavian migrants in their 'front' region of Stuttgart, Germany. The station is their regular meeting place. (From J. Berger and J. Mohr, *A Seventh Man*, Writers and Readers Publishing Cooperative, London, 1982. Courtesy of Jean Mohr.)

perspectives offered by Marxists cannot be rejected. People must find work in order to subsist. On the other hand, capitalist economies are based on the willing and active involvement of the very workers they are exploiting.

Something is taking place which is enabling capitalist economies in this way. We suggest here that moral careers (the preservation of reputation) and the protection and preservation of kin offer as much if not more explanation of local social systems and the mobility of workers as those emphasising class and class struggle. To put this another way, the biological and emotional mechanisms outlined in Chapter 1 are just as important as the circuit of capital in affecting social and spatial change. The two are clearly combining with one another.

NOTES AND REFERENCES

1. F. Frobel, J. Heinrichs and O. Kreye (1980) *The New International Division of Labour*, Cambridge University Press. D. Massey (1984) *Spatial Divisions of Labour*, Macmillan, London.
2. The word 'services' is widely used, but often with little exactitude. A useful set of distinctions is between (a) service *industries* involving, for example, the making and selling of an intangible product such as a meal in a restaurant, (b) service *occupations* in the public and private sectors, (c) service *functions*: the specific uses that people derive from industrial products as well as from the service industries and occupations. See J. Urry (1985) 'Deindustrialisation, households and politics', in L. Murgatroyd, M. Savage, D. Shapiro, S. Walby, A. Warde, J. Mark-Lawson, *Localities, Class and Gender*, Pion, London.
3. D. Harvey (1982) *The Limits to Capital*, Blackwell, Oxford.
4. On the return of capital to Europe see P. Dickens (1988) *One Nation?*, Pluto, London, chapter 3.
5. F. Frobel *et al.* (1980) op. cit., p. 405.
6. F. Frobel *et al.* (1980) op. cit., pp. 405–406.
7. D. Harvey (1985) 'The geopolitics of capitalism', in D. Gregory and J. Urry (eds), *Social Relations and Spatial Structures*, Macmillan, London.
8. D. Harvey (1985) ibid., p. 151.
9. B. Warren (1979) *Imperialism: Pioneer of Capitalism*, Verso, London.
10. B. Warren (1979) ibid., p. 253.
11. B. Warren (1979) ibid., p. xiii.
12. B. Warren (1979) ibid., p. xiii.
13. This argument is made by J. Urry in his influential paper 'Localities, regions and social class', *International Journal of Urban and Regional Research*, 5 (4) 1981.

14. K. Morgan and A. Sayer (1988) *Microcircuits of Capital*, Polity, Oxford.

15. M. Savage (1988) 'The missing link? The relationship between spatial mobility and social mobility', *British Journal of Sociology*, **XXIX** (4).

16. J. Goldthorpe, C. Llewellyn and C. Payne (1987) *Social Mobility and Class Structure in Modern Britain* (2nd edn), Oxford University Press, Oxford.

17. W. Whyte (1957) *The Organization Man*, Cape, London.

18. On fragmentations within the service class and differential levels of spatial mobility see P. Dickens (1988) op. cit., and M. Savage, P. Dickens and A. Fielding (1988) 'Some social and political implications of the contemporary fragmentation of the "service class" in Britain', *International Journal of Urban and Regional Research*, **12** (3).

19. For a discussion of declining spatial mobility and its implications see P. Dickens (1988) op. cit. and Savage *et al.* (1988) op. cit.

20. R. Cohen (1987) *The New Helots*, Avebury, Aldershot.

21. E. Mandel (1978) *Late Capitalism*, Verso, London.

22. E. Mandel (1978) ibid., p. 170.

23. M. Burawoy (1979) *Manufacturing Consent*, Chicago University Press, Chicago.

24. H. Beynon (1984) *Working for Ford*, Pelican, Harmondsworth.

25. On the creation of back regions by workers attempting to protect their class and male identity see also C. Cockburn (1983) *Brothers*, Pluto Press, London, pp. 108 seq.

26. J. Davis (1973) *Land and Family in Pisticci*, Athlone Press, London.

27. J. Davis (1973) ibid., p. 160.

28. J. Davis (1973) ibid., p. 171.

29. J. Davis (1973) ibid., p. 73.

30. J. Davis (1973) ibid., pp. 64–5.

31. J. Davis (1973) ibid., p. 24.

32. Davis writes of the typical Pisticcian home in the following way: 'The front space is also used for display. Refrigerators, television sets, elegant modern gas-cookers with their glass-fronted ovens filled with the family's most ornate best coffee cups . . . are common sights.

   In the back are the sleeping quarters: the matrimonial bed covered with a day-time bedspread, and smaller beds or couches for children, a dressing table, two bedside tables, at least one wardrobe . . . and the large chest in which linen is kept.' (pp. 5–6)

33. J. Davis (1973) ibid., p. 94.

34. J. Davis (1973) ibid., p. 94.

35. J. Berger and J. Mohr (1982) *A Seventh Man*, Writers and Readers Publishing Cooperative, London.

36. J. Berger and J. Mohr (1982) ibid., p. 23.

37. J. Berger and J. Mohr (1982) ibid., p. 29.

38. J. Berger and J. Mohr (1982) ibid., p. 115.

39. J. Berger and J. Mohr (1982) ibid., p. 118.
40. J. Berger and J. Mohr (1982) ibid., p. 221.
41. J. Berger and J. Mohr (1982) ibid., p. 224.
42. J. Berger and J. Mohr (1982) ibid., p. 225.

4

CIVIL SOCIETY, ESCAPE ATTEMPTS AND SELF-DETERMINATION

In Chapter 1 we argued that conscious awareness, the images and representations that people use to communicate with each other and the various forms of deliberate planning and foresight which they use are all partly a result of the myriad social relationships in which they are caught up, and partly a product of deep-rooted instincts and emotions. As Figure 1.2 (p. 12) also shows, however, consciousness awareness is also a product of what Harré *et al.* call 'behavioural routines': the raising of a voice to be heard, for example, or spontaneous reaction to danger.

Harré *et al.* argue that for the social sciences a key research priority should also be an improved understanding of the deep-rooted social and instinctive relationships and processes to which the conscious aspects of the mind are subjected. Their understanding of social action is a 'realist' one, in so far as they believe there to be general, deep-lying mechanisms affecting human conduct which are triggered in different ways by contingent social circumstances. The realist approach to explanation is one that we discuss further and use in Chapter 6. Harré *et al.* further suggest, as Figure 1.2 also implies, that the deep structures and instincts of the mind have evolved in relation to the social processes and relations in which human beings have developed.

Tantalisingly, Harré *et al.* argue that both of these processes at the 'top' level of the human mind (level 3 of Figure 1.2) have yet to be properly understood. Furthermore, they argue that the crucial relationships *between* them have remained almost entirely unexplored. On the one hand, we have social scientists offering their understanding of the social structures and processes affecting people's behaviour. On the other, we have psychologists, ethologists and sociobiologists offering their understanding of individual and collective behaviour. But how do these interact to influence our thought and behaviour? How do such interactions relate to our special interest in locality and space?

These questions demand great research effort. At this stage we can make only tentative suggestions. A key first step is to remember Harré *et al.*'s 'realist' starting point. In Chapter 1 we found psychologists, biologists and ethologists making far-reaching claims for socially unmediated, innate drives affecting people's lives. Territoriality, male (and juvenile) aggressiveness, the demand for property, the protection and preservation of kin, and an innate need for ontological security were all put forward as being at the core of individual and social behaviour and observable in unmediated form in people's behaviour.

All these biological and psychological imperatives will continue to be much argued over. The point is, however, that they combine with, and are mediated by, the social world. So it is misleading to suggest, as many psychologists and sociobiologists are prone to do, that these mechanisms are necessarily *the* prime mechanism affecting awareness and action. As we discuss in Chapter 6, a better way to envisage such imperatives is as *latent*: waiting, as it were, to be activated by the social and political relations and contexts in which people are living.

What has this to do with our central theme of locality? People, of course, live in a number of different kinds of social relations and contexts. And, despite the fact that employment is a means by which personal and social respect can be gained, it offers relatively few prospects for the presentation of 'self' as a unique individual. The mobility of capital, combined with the overriding demands for profit-making and profitability, severely limit the extent to which people's innate needs for self-realisation at the workplace and their control over capital investment in the locality where they live can be satisfied. Arguably, however, this extends more to those in relatively menial and unskilled tasks and less to those high-flying executives who are able to combine the need for social identity, sexual fulfilment and the like with the profitability of their enterprises.

When we come to civil society, though, the possibilities for a much wider group of people are rather different. Civil society is constituted by the social relationships and processes outside paid employment and not immediately affected by the state. As used by Marxists, the concept refers to the circulation of capital, with people exchanging the money they have earned in employment for the goods and services they need and require. It refers also to the reproduction of the labour force. People must turn up at the proverbial factory gates fresh, fit and ready to toil. A recovery process must take place: in the home, the pub or elsewhere in the surrounding locality. It is at this point that we can make our first connection with the emphases we have laid out at the beginning of this book. Civil society is the prime context of biological reproduction, the raising of future generations and the support of kin.

For now what seem rather obscure reasons, much of 'urban' sociology has taken the form of the sociology of civil society or of consumption. There is no self-evident reason for continuing to insist that urban sociology should be equated with consumption or civil society, interesting as these areas of study are. But there are good reasons for examining how self-realisation and moral careers are developed within civil society. As Marx himself argued, the sphere of social life outside employment is indeed where the individual labourer has the best chance of achieving some degree of identity, autonomy and control over his or her life. And as Harré implies (citing Veblen in his support), there is growing evidence that, in more affluent societies, questions of display and possessions outside paid work are of growing significance to the formation of people's self-esteem and recognition by others. Here, then, is the second way in which we can connect the Marxist or political economy perspectives on urban sociology to our particular interest in human nature. Civil society provides, perhaps, the key means by which deep-rooted emotional drives can be realised. It is replete with prospects for 'escape attempts'; zones of autonomy and self-expression separate from employment and not regulated by state authority.

So in turning to social processes outside employment, we are shifting to a sphere of study which has been well trodden by urban sociology. Paradoxically, however, our enthusiasm in turning to these processes lies more in examining how questions of identity and moral careers come to be formed rather than in continuing to equate 'urban' with 'consumption' or 'social reproduction'.

This chapter is organised along the following lines. Firstly it will briefly trace how urban sociology came to be equated with questions of consumption. However, it will also show how recent developments within the definition of the 'urban', as it applies to consumption, are now indeed beginning to touch on our central concerns. Civil society is a necessarily diverse sphere of social life. It is, however, possible to thematise it around dominant and subordinate forms of social life. Here we explore what appears to be an emergent way of life entitled 'postmodern'; one associated particularly with the middle classes. Secondly, we turn to the question of lifestyles led by subordinate social groups and their relationship to the home. The intention throughout is again to demonstrate how conventional urban sociology might be combined with the new approaches outlined at the beginning of this study.

URBAN SOCIOLOGY AS THE SOCIOLOGY OF CONSUMPTION: SOME THEMES AND DEBATES

The elision between urban sociology and the sociology of consumption started with Manuel Castells's early work. Writing as a Marxist influenced by the philosopher Louis Althusser, Castells argued that urban sociology, especially that developed by the Chicago School, was 'ideological'.[1] By this he meant that urban sociologists had never stopped to ask what was actually theoretically significant about cities and city life. What, Castells asked, does 'urban' or 'city' life actually mean? The Chicago School, as we have seen, argued that there actually was some characteristic feature of the 'urban way of life': one entailing separation and isolation of people from one another and thereby generating crime and social disorder. Castells challenged this, arguing that there was, in fact, no such thing as an 'urban' sociology.

The 'ideology' of existing urban sociology stemmed, he argued, from the fact that analysis never stopped to examine the underlying factors affecting these supposedly 'urban' effects; unemployment, for example, or bad housing. For a Marxist, this of course meant that class relations and the processes underlying capital accumulation received no systematic attention. 'Ideology', for Castells, does not necessarily mean that the Chicago School is in an absolute sense 'wrong'. It means that this type of analysis lights upon a particular aspect of social life and social change (and an aspect of life with which Chicagoans were immediately concerned in the 1920s) without attending to what Castells or a structuralist Marxist would see as the principal underlying processes affecting people's lives, especially economic processes and those related to the social relations of production.

So Castells proposed a wholly new definition of what 'urban' sociology consists of. Writing in the late 1960s and early 1970s, he argued that advanced capitalist societies were caught up in a major contradiction. Capital, if it is to remain profitable, needed its workforce constantly reproduced. That is to say, houses, hospitals, schools and so forth were needed to reproduce a workforce which had the capacity and ability to engage in labour.

Yet the contradiction as seen by Castells was that capital, if it was to remain profitable, could not afford to provide such facilities itself. This meant that 'collective consumption' had to be provided, mediated by the state. The state according to Castells's perspective, had the central role of ensuring a healthy capitalist economy. It is, therefore, obliged by capitalist firms to provide these facilities itself. The costs of such facilities are, however, spread over the population as a whole. So, henceforth, 'urban' sociology would concern itself with the provision of such collective facilities. As such it was to become inextricably bound up with a number of conflicts surrounding such provision.

These tensions stemmed, Castells argued, from the fact that as states intervened, these items of collective consumption become highly politicised. Through mounting intervention to sustain a profitable economy, capitalist states are haphazardly establishing a wholly new arena of political confrontation. Castells, much of whose work was based on France in the late 1960s, argued that new kinds of social and political alliances were being organised around collective consumption. Working class people, for example, were combining with public sector workers to ensure that such collective provision was in fact provided.

At the same time, however, these so-called urban social movements represented in Castells's eyes a threat to the state and its spending. Governments were under constant pressure to provide such facilities and, in addition to politicising consumption, they constantly risked running into fiscal crises themselves or charging even higher taxes on the capitalist enterprises they were supposed to be supporting. In short, capitalist states were becoming thoroughly entangled in a set of conflicts from which they could not easily extricate themselves. Castells's new definition of the 'urban' was therefore dedicated to understanding this new, complex and highly visible form of social conflict.

Seen in retrospect, Castells's work seems as bound in time and place as the Chicago School itself. As events since the early 1970s have shown, many advanced capitalist states have in fact had much less trouble than anticipated in extricating themselves from the provision of collective consumption. In Britain, for example, successive governments have managed to almost wholly withdraw from the provision of public sector housing. So the contradiction identified by Castells turned out much less problematic and insoluble than imagined.

This problem of theory being tied to particular historical and social contexts relates closely to two other concerns linked with Castells's work. First is the fact that his capitalist society seemed to consist of mechanisms and relationships with universal effects throughout capitalism. French, British, Swedish and American capitalism, for example, were all seen as forced to adopt similar strategies as a result of similar underlying economic forces and contradictions. Yet we can now see that Castells's all-embracing theory could never have been straightforwardly extended to the particular kinds of class and social relations constituting particular societies and localities. Secondly, despite Castells's emphasis on imminent urban social movements, very little attention was given to the nature of human agency. People, their understandings of their circumstances and their struggles to force collective facilities out of the state, were again under-conceptualised and, indeed, even seemed to have a small role to play.

One final point of criticism. For many sociologists and geographers, the equation of the 'urban' with 'consumption' seemed unnecessarily restrictive. Why, as urban sociologists such as those we reviewed in the last chapter argued, should a spatial or urban sociology not also be concerned with the class relations of production?

Castells's pioneering work did much to question underlying assumptions and, for better or worse, break the mould of the old urban sociology. The above criticisms of his work seemed quite comprehensive, and to Castells's credit, he largely agreed with them. Indeed, by the early 1980s Castells had largely rejected the kind of grand theorising he had earlier been proposing. The result was an urban sociology which came very close to that which we have been developing in this book. Castells's rejection of his old view took place with his *City and the Grassroots*, published in 1983.[2] His emphasis on 'urban social movements' remained; indeed the reasons for the success or failure of such movements is the key theme of his book. He also maintained his interest in collective consumption in so far as he argued that a successful urban social movement must articulate a demand for that kind of state-provided facility.

The City and the Grassroots argued, on the other hand, that successful urban social movements must confront state domination (the tendency being for such domination to be centralised and tied up with the interests of monopoly capital) and recognise the nature of local culture and experience. This latter item was of special importance to the Castells of the early 1980s. It represented his growing recognition that social change is created not just through the inevitable and impersonal workings of capitalist societies, but by the experience, understanding (and hence the demands) gained by people in their everyday lives in the limited spatial context of their localities. At the same time, he sees many urban social movements as defensive, insular and failing to challenge the deeper structures of society and state power.

Castells gives as an example the gay community in San Francisco. On the one hand, their very colonisation of an inner urban area and their resistance to major urban renewal was a way in which their collective and personal identities were asserted. The property and land markets were shaped towards their own ends. On the other hand, this group's demands remain quite narrow. It did not mount a sustained challenge against globally-organised capitalism, concentrated state power or even prevailing discrimination against homosexuals. The result was what Castells called a 'local utopia'; one constrained to a small locality and an alternative culture and not substantially challenging state power.

So Castells was the pioneer of what came to be seen as the 'new urban sociology' and, paradoxically, *The City and the Grassroots* seemed to recover some of the themes (especially that of the experience of the immediate spatial and social setting) which he had earlier rejected in the Chicago School. Castells has now moved on to new areas of research, one of these being new forms of communications technology and the threats and opportunities represented by such developments.[3] Meanwhile, however, his emphasis on consumption set the tone for a very thriving area of urban sociology by later writers in this tradition.

Despite the fact, then, that Castells has now moved to other concerns, consumption and civil society remain key themes in urban sociology. Castells's interest in the politics of consumption and the political alliances surrounding consumption have, for example, been developed by Dunleavy.[4] In a number of influential papers he has argued that people's political alignments are closely connected to their relationships to the state. And these relationships to the state are, he argues, largely supplanting their class in determining their politics.

He demonstrates, for example, that the British Labour Party was most likely to find support not simply from the working class but from that sector of the working class which still strongly relied on collective provision. Furthermore, such a group was likely to find allies amongst public sector workers who depended on the state for their incomes. Indeed, one of Dunleavy's key themes is the central role of state professionals and bureaucracies defending their own material positions, if necessary at the expense of the public services they are supposed to be providing. We, nevertheless, postpone consideration of the state until the next chapter.

EXPLAINING AN EMERGENT FORM OF DOMINANT CULTURE

Urban sociology has tended recently to turn its attention away from the politics of collective consumption and towards a wider debate regarding the changing nature of civil society. It is now frequently argued that advanced capitalist societies are moving into a wholly new form of 'postmodern' culture. Futhermore, the spatial aspects of this culture are seen as having a special significance.

What is postmodern culture? Why has it emerged? What has it to do with the 'urban'? These are difficult questions to answer despite the great rush of recent material on this matter. Indeed, much of the literature on postmodernism seems programatically aimed at avoiding an explanation of what 'it' actually is. 'It' seems to have a number of facets. Indeed, one of its defining characteristics is its lack of a single 'discourse' or theory.

Nevertheless, let us, at least, start with what it is and how it might be explained. All forms of culture entail communications through images, language and signs. The idea of a postmodern culture refers, however, to a way of life in which signs and forms of communication have largely become separated from content and from the specific contexts in which they are being projected and received. Jean Baudrillard, one of the leading commentators on postmodernist culture, sees America as the society where postmodernism has most fully developed.[5] Here is one instance of a sign or message being separated from emotion or content. Baudrillard is describing what might be called a 'have a nice day' culture:

They certainly smile at you here, though neither from courtesy, nor from an effort to charm. This smile signifies only the need. It is a bit like the Cheshire Cat's grin: it continues to float on faces long after all emotion had disappeared. A smile available at any moment, but half-scared to exist, to give itself away. No ulterior motive lurks behind it, but it keeps you at a distance.[6]

A central idea of postmodernism is, therefore, that appearances do not correspond to reality; reality in the above case being the actual emotions and feelings transmitted and interpreted. The expressive order, it is argued, has become the message itself, with 'back' emotions exploding out to the 'front'. The whole of social life, it is argued, has become 'flat'. In our terms, there are no backs and no fronts. Postmodern culture therefore entails, according to Jameson, 'a new depthlessness' with feeling, emotion and subjectivity vanishing from human communication and parody, mannerism, and pastiche taking their place. In these ways, superficiality and surface appearances have replaced authenticity, emotional depth and true feelings.

Postmodern sociology, as outlined by Baudrillard, Lyotard and other commentators such as Jameson and Davis, is said to possess a number of other related features.[7] Perhaps the most important is the abandonment of single 'truths', theories or discourses. Similarly, postmodern culture is also seen as highly diverse and mass produced. Indeed, postmodern culture is envisaged as entailing and celebrating 'the death of the author'; the abandonment of products surrounded with the aura of creation and uniqueness and attributable to charismatic producers. Pastiche and lack of originality in popular culture is therefore seen as the result. Baudrillard goes even further than this by suggesting that the whole of contemporary life is dedicated to consumption and communication in a way which has become wholly disconnected from meaning and content. Again, the argument is that social life, particularly in the advanced societies such as the USA, is led at the increasingly superficial level of appearances and utterances.

Why has this form of culture developed? The explanations are various and, as I argue shortly, rather limited. For Baudrillard and Lyotard postmodern culture is largely free-floating, with little contact with social relations and processes. Jameson and Davis recognise, however, that it is somehow linked with developments in capitalism itself. Capitalism is creating these superficial images. Meaning is being marketed. Emotions, feelings and aesthetics are all being increasingly commodified. Theories of postmodernism, therefore, relate the emergence of this type of culture with changes in capitalist economy and the rapid penetration of market relations into all aspects of personal and social life. This applies especially to the life of the more affluent, most of whom are concentrated in the advanced societies.

Jameson, Harvey, and Lash and Urry argue, albeit with rather different emphases, that the emergence of postmodernism corresponds to a new phase in capitalist development. They suggest that 'modern' aesthetics and culture were associated with mass production, with state bureaucracies treating individuals as standard products, and with a form of capitalism not yet fully operating at a global scale. By contrast,

postmodern culture and aesthetics are associated with the globally-
organised production of commodities and with 'flexible' forms of
manufacturing rapidly adapting to ever-changing forms of market
demands from the increasingly affluent societies of the advanced industrial world. Similarly, the decline of the welfare state means that people
are increasingly treated as private citizens or defined by gender, race,
religion and 'class fractions' rather than as standard 'people' with
standard needs.

Lash and Urry argue that postmodern culture nevertheless particularly
benefits the 'service class' of senior white collar workers: a group which is
given special attention in Chapter 1. This is because a socially and
economically dominant group is best able to engage in and control all
aspects of contemporary culture, setting norms and values for others.

These arguments have strong implications for our special interests in
locality and locale. They also link up well with our conceptual starting-
points. For the middle classes in particular, everyday life and human
association is increasingly dedicated to Veblenesque display. Commodities are purchased not for their use values but as signs and symbols to
emphasise personal and social distinctiveness. Part of such display takes
place through the design of locales. Contemporary architecture, for
example, is increasingly abstracted from the social and spatial contexts in
which it is constructed. Postmodern towers, in Davis's words are 'a
package of standardised space gift wrapped for the client's taste'. The
external elevations of one skyscraper in London's docklands, for example,
takes a 'Neo Gothic' form. Meanwhile, a recently completed tower in
New York is based on early nineteenth century designs for Chippendale
furniture.[8] Postmodern design therefore, emphasises difference and distinction. But the resulting variety is literally *skin-deep*.

This brings us back once more to the personal and social implications
of such developments. Despite all the apparent difference of contemporary design and culture, everyday experience is increasingly detached
from local cultures and social relations.

The Marxist, class-based, explanations of this emergent postmodern
culture are certainly valuable. Yet despite their insistence on a new form
of human experience (one which is curiously reminiscent of the early
sociologists' insistence that late nineteenth and early twentieth societies
were emerging into a new society which was leaving behind *gemeinschaft*
relations of blood and community) it is somewhat surprising to find that
contemporary postmodern theorists give only schematic attention to
human consciousness and agency. They also become unnecessarily entan-

gled in the issue of when the new form of culture actually became dominant. Is it now? Was it in the 1960s? Is there not plenty of evidence of pastiche and parody in earlier, supposedly 'modernist', times? This issue is, however, symptomatic of a deeper problem of explanation; one to which we can now turn.

As we have discussed, there is now available a conceptual framework for adequately understanding the changing nature of contemporary civil society. Reference should again be made to Figures 1.1 and 1.2 (pages 11 and 12) and our elaborations of Harré *et al.*'s framework as a means of explaining postmodern culture.

Lash and Urry are amongst the few commentators we have reviewed who recognise that the middle classes are those best able to indulge in, and benefit by, this emergent form of culture. But analysis has so far been largely entrapped by the particular form of Marxism with which cultural theory has adopted. Armed with the suggestions of Harré, Veblen and others we can now see that postmodernism is not simply a product of capital movements or recent developments in the industrial economy such as consumer-led, 'flexible', forms of production. It is simultaneously the products of increasingly affluent individuals and households attempting to establish identity, uniqueness and esteem in their own eyes and those of others.

People do this, as Veblen argued in relation to the American middle classes about a century ago, through various forms of conspicuous consumption and display. And typically the forms used for such display are versions of the cultural forms adopted and displayed by the ruling classes. In this sense they are usually 'appropriating' the form displayed in the public realm by the affluent, pace-setting reference groups. The precise timing of this process is largely irrelevant. Veblen saw it developing in late twentieth century America. And in Chapter 2 we saw G. H. Mead and the Chicago School of Sociology recognising how people used reference groups as a means of establishing their personal identities. Clearly, this process has developed considerably during the late twentieth century. As we discuss shortly, Bourdieu's work shows these processes of emulation to be combined with the extraordinarily subtle means by which social groups also distinguish themselves from each other. And to the extent that the form of the middle class varies between localities and societies, these dominant social groups presumably have quite different effects on local cultures. Admittedly, however, such variations remain largely unresearched.

The cultural forms adopted by the rising middle classes (or, more specifically, Lash and Urry's 'service class') cannot be the 'real thing.' Only so many people can actually live in a real farmhouse or Elizabethan manor. Indeed, they would probably not wish to do so unless it was centrally heated. Only so many can engage at leisure with Indian or Mexican society. For the rest of us it is a commercially 'packaged' version of the real thing. If we understand people as continually persisting in what we have earlier termed 'identity projects' it need come as no surprise to find increasingly affluent households necessarily consuming pastiche, the extraction of history out of context, and superficiality as a normal way of life. All this, however, in the search for social esteem and personal uniqueness.

Theorists of postmodernism relying on political economy explanations still do not adequately explain why sections of the middle class are engaging in this new way of life. Bourdieu's work on the new middle classes (what he calls the new petit bourgeoisie) and Goldthorpe *et al.*'s study of the service class's social mobility provide us with some clues.[9] These people work mainly in the new, rapidly growing, employment sectors such as personal services, advertising and the media. They are socially mobile, many of them having risen from working class backgrounds to new heights in the class structure. They have a socially diverse array of friends and colleagues, some of them 'old' working class friends but many of them in circumstances similar to those in which they now find themselves. They have thereby developed few class allegiances and few commitments to large-scale theories about how society is, or should be, organised. Their commitment is to a culture of individual success and a highly hedonistic view of life. In one of Bourdieu's many memorable turns of phrase, they suffer from 'fear of not getting enough pleasure'.[10]

Bourdieu and Goldthorpe give us some preliminary insights into why a a particularly dominant social group should engage in a postmodern way of life; one which stems from social mobility, high incomes and which largely sets the pace for the remainder of the population. But there may well be even more subtle reasons why this group should find itself attracted to this particular form of civil society. Class positions and economic power may again be only a limited part of the explanation.

Pfeil makes the acute and useful observation that many of these individuals were raised in households where the father failed to make a significant impact on their offspring's development; a product of increasing household dissolution amongst the middle classes.[11] The result, he argues, is that many middle class children have never progressed beyond the 'pre-Oedipal phase'. As we have seen earlier, this is a Freudian term implying that they are still committed to the 'pleasure principle'. Oral and anal pleasure and satisfaction remain their primary instincts while the 'normal' identification with the authoritarian father-figure enforcing codes of discipline has never occurred. Again, therefore, explanation entails a combination of the economic or social processes familiar to sociology (and urban sociology) with mechanisms which lie deep within people's biological and psychological makeup.

SUBORDINATE CULTURES: TOWARDS A MORE COMPLEX EXPLANATION

We now turn from dominant to subordinate cultures in civil society. The latter are amongst the 'back' activities outlined earlier as characteristically taking place in 'back regions'. What Cohen calls the 'new subcultural theory' needs first putting in a wider context. If class is to be the starting-point then we must recognise that there are a number of different subcultures, many organised around groups of young people, but with ethnicity forming another important dimension. Here we give special attention to youth. Ethnicity is given more extended treatment in the following chapters.

Firstly, the placing of the new subcultural theory relating to youth in a somewhat wider context. As Yablonsky argues, subordinate gangs can be defined in three ways.[12] One type adopts and aspires to dominant middle class values and priorities. A second 'delinquent' type is one in which the gang still broadly aspires to dominant ideas of success (including the equation of 'success' with material rewards) but finds alternative means towards these ends. Hence the reliance on what is socially defined as 'crime' and various forms of illegal profits. Thirdly, there is the potentially violent gang. This is self-aggrandising and largely relies on defining its own culture through outright conflicts with other subgroups and the dominant social order. It is the third and possibly the second group to which 'new subcultural theory' applies.

A second assumption which needs challenging, however, is this work's continuing and immense emphasis on class theory. Such an emphasis leaves the analysis constrained by its relatively narrow conceptual framework.[13] Class-based mechanisms are again, therefore, seen as the main mechanism explaining the emergence of subcultures, and what are called 'hooliganism' and 'juvenile deliquency'. The young working class in deindustrialising, inner urban areas are seen by the new subcultural theory as caught up in a bitter series of conflicts and contradictions. Urban redevelopment has transformed the inner urban areas where working class adolescents have been raised. Skilled manual labour has largely disappeared, jobs are temporary and badly paid, and unemployment has rapidly increased as capital has removed elsewhere.[14] Meanwhile, the upwardly mobile members of this generation (Yablonsky's first group) have dispersed to the front regions of respectable parts of the city.

According to Cohen (and, indeed, to related work such as that outlined by Hebdidge) subcultural or gang life should be envisaged as resistance to these changes and forms of social subordination.[15] They argue that working class adolescents are, in fact, creating a collective, close-knit, community life which is a re-establishment of traditional working class cultures and values. Nevertheless, the material fact is, of course, that capital has largely abandoned these inner urban areas. Resistance by working class youth, therefore, takes various 'magical' or 'symbolic' forms: dress, style, alternative ways of life.

Territory has a particular kind of significance in all this in so far as these young people are reasserting their lost solidarity and independence through literally 'winning space': claiming particular territories to be 'theirs'. In the terms discussed in Chapter 2 during our reinterpretation of the Chicago School, these groups convert certain districts in what for them are front regions. For other social groups, however, they may well be seen as back regions to be avoided.

The important point for the contemporary literature on subcultures is that this type of resistance through rituals is still 'symbolic'. The ways in which old working class identity is re-formed still relies on cultural forms. 'Alternative' forms of subculture are still very much adaptations of dominant cultural forms: language and other modes of expression being, for example, adaptations of those generally, publicly, or commercially available. Similarly, patriarchal relations between men and women or racism are also a frequent feature of these supposedly alternative forms of gang life.

So the general point about this literature is that oppositional youth cultures amongst working class youth are still envisaged as closely linked not just to wider public values but to *middle class* public values. Meanwhile, however, dominant forms of culture (the fragmented, superficial and commercialised postmodernism we discussed earlier) seem to take up and incorporate many of these forms of resistance relatively easy; albeit in sanitised, respectable, forms.

Again, however, if we recall the biological and psychological concepts discussed in Chapters 1 and 2, this overarching emphasis on class seems unnecessarily limiting. More specifically, it gives little attention to processes other than those related to class (including 'lost' class) experience and the demands of capital accumulation. At the same time it tends to overlook the accounts and understandings of the people actively engaged in 'subcultural' ways of life.

In trying to explain the territorial behaviour and sporadic violence of young working class people, for example, one approach would be to take much more seriously the currently unfashionable ethological and biological literature we reviewed in Chapter 1. Lorenz and Ardrey suggest, respectively, that aggression and territoriality form a deep-lying part of people's biological and psychic constitution.[16]

As outlined earlier, Tiger and Fox suggest that there is an innate 'male bonding' stemming from millions of years' history and ultimately linked to a time when men co-operated in order to hunt.[17] Young male groups in primitive societies are seen as early proof of the formation of co-operative groups in which individuals learn to work in the interests of the wider group. Clearly, group formation and aggression by contemporary human beings has little to do with hunting and survival. Lorenz, Ardrey and others nevertheless argue that collective instincts and forms of aggression amongst contemporary human beings (and especially amongst males) have now been canalised into ritual and symbolic forms: types of aggression which do not usually result in damage.

If we turn to the literature which attempts to combine sociobiology with social psychology, we find the formation of youth subcultures being given an explanation which is largely at odds with that proposed by Marxism. Basing his analysis on a combination of Freud and genetics, Badcock argues that young people forming oppositional, 'alternative' cultures are, in fact, resisting the oppressive emotional investment of their parents.[18] Contemporary societies, he argues, are characterised by relatively small families. As a result, biological and psychological investment by parents is being invested in a relatively small number of children. The result is that young adults, themselves seeking a separate sexual and personal identity, are resisting the way of life lived and promoted by their parents. State authorities attempting to regulate youth culture are seen as little more than parent substitutes. The upshot of this work is, then, that the term 'parent culture' used by Marxists needs to be taken more seriously.

Yet the danger of both these kinds of literature is that they offer just the kinds of all-explaining and deterministic theories as the form of Marxism we reviewed earlier. Categories of behaviour such as 'territoriality' and 'aggression' are first lumped together in an unproblematic way. Secondly, they are given simple, catch-all explanations. Furthermore, territoriality, violence (including violence towards women and children) and all forms of resistance can be all too readily justified as *simply* 'natural' and 'innate'.

In addressing this literature we are clearly involved in some extremely tricky judgements and issues. But, as regards the formation of youth subcultures with an occasional tendency to violence, a way forward is offered by Marsh, Rosser and Harré in their study of a particular form of youth subculture: football 'hooliganism'.[19] In line with their realist view of human behaviour, they suggest that there are indeed latent forms of behaviour within the biological makeup of human beings. The crucial point is again, however, that they *are* only latent. It takes specific cultural processes and relationships to, as it were, spark off these latent tendencies. Marsh *et al.* are particularly interested in the aggression of 'hooligans' on the football terraces. As they put it 'the actual arousal of aggression would seem to be very much a cultural affair'.[20]

We could make a similar point about the psychological literature explaining subculture as resistance to parental norms. 'Difficult teenagers' are, for parents and children alike, an almost universal problem. But how 'difficult' they are, the form these difficulties take, perhaps even whether they are difficult at all, must again be a 'cultural affair'. Presumably the actual outcome depends on, for example, the social classes of the people involved, and the kinds of resistance they encounter from parents and other authorities. This takes us back to Yablonsky's useful distinctions. As he suggests, biological and psychological imperatives may well take different forms. It may even be, if the young people involved broadly adopt the 'parent' culture, that they turn out not to be imperatives at all. The implications are again that any analysis must attempt the difficult task of combining the kinds of analysis offered by sociology with those offered by psychology and biology.

The second main point about Marsh *et al.*'s approach is that it recognises the expressive order: the theories which young people and others have about their circumstances. Theories, of course, lie behind their behaviour. Underlying the behaviour of an apparently undifferentiated and chaotic mass of hooligans are distinct rules and moral careers. The young football supporters talked to by these authors have their own, mutually understood, hierarchies and regulations. Indeed, many of these tacit rules remind us of those examined by the Chicago School in their early studies of youth gangs.

At the 'top' are the Town Boys, a group of older boys and young men who, while not waving banners or making the most noise, are nevertheless treated in a deferential way by other subgroups. Beneath them are The Rowdies, a group of boys aged between 12 and 17. They make the most noise: singing, chanting and consistently insulting opposing supporters. This second group is what the mass media usually refer to as 'hooligans'. Beneath them are a group of children with an average age of 10. They are the Novices, sometimes dubbed 'little kids' by the older and superior supporters. In fact, the hierarchy is even more complex than this, with individual Rowdies, for example, being Aggro Leaders. But the general point is that this hierarchy represents a ladder up which 'lower' groups aspire to climb. But this is a result of those at the top of the hierarchy maintaining their status amongst their subordinates. As Marsh *et al.* put it:

'Becoming somebody' is a highly structured affair, and an understanding of this structure is the first step in rendering the apparently anomic behaviour at football matches intelligible.[21]

Furthermore, these social differences have a spatial expression, each group occupying distinct if overlapping regions of the football terrace (Figure 4.1).

Marsh *et al.*'s study of football hooligans and their emphasis on the expressive order has some similarities with other studies of 'counter-cultures'. Especially well known is Willis's *Learning to Labour*, a study of cultures which working class children construct for themselves at school.[22] Some boys, 'the lads', represent outright opposition to school culture, its rules and hierarchies. Their school life is largely dedicated to preventing themselves being educated. This is done through innumerable forms of minor subversion, tricks and escape attempts within the school routine. Willis is at pains to point out, however, that this breaking of rules not only relies on having the rules there to break but ensures that 'the lads' condemn themselves to the worst jobs once they have left school. Meanwhile, 'the earoles' are the 'respectable' students who obey the rules, get the better jobs but remain low down in the schoolchildren's own counter-culture.

Willis is, in effect, tracing the moral career of small groups of children; this time from the school into their place of employment. His book again shows locales being used as a resource in this process, 'the lads' using

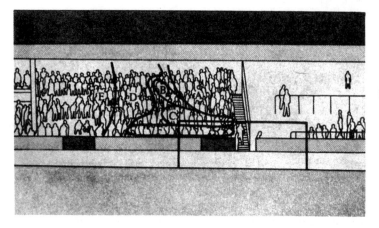

Figure 4.1 Moral careers and subordinate culture: the spatial distribution of home fans at Oxford United Football Club. A – The Rowdies, B – intermediate group, C – the Town Boys, D – heterogeneous group (older), E – heterogeneous group (younger), F – novices. (From P. Marsh *et al.*, *The Rules of Disorder*, Routledge, London, 1978. Reproduced with permission.)

distinct rooms and spaces to literally separate themselves from school authorities, from the 'earoles' and from the much-despised Pakistanis and West Indians.

Two summary points can be made about dominant and subordinate cultures. One is to repeat the perhaps obvious point concerning the relationships between these spheres of social life. 'Front' cultures have a way of incorporating apparent resistances and incorporating them into forms compatible with the established social order. Meanwhile 'back' cultures are often a distorted version of dominant forms. The structures common to society as a whole (especially the structure of language) do not simply constrain alternative values and ways of life. They also provide the resources around which alternatives are constructed. Paradoxically, both dominant and subordinate seem to sustain each other in a reciprocal fashion. Secondly, we have been trying to develop an understanding of locality in human agency; one responsive not only to social or cultural processes but also to instinctive demands and human interaction. We can now develop both these points by turning to a particular important aspect of civil society: the home.

DOMINANT CULTURES, SUBORDINATE CULTURES, INSTINCTS AND THE HOME

A fascinating feature of Castells's legacy is that later authors have continued to examine the sphere of reproduction and consumption despite the facts that Castells's original theories have emerged as far less universally applicable than he suggested and that many of his followers are not Marxists. The reasons for this are clear if we examine the work of two well known urban sociologists, Pahl and Saunders. For them a central reason for concentrating on civil society lies in the social and emotional significance of the home.

Pahl, in his *Divisions of Labour*, argues strongly that a rapidly decreasing proportion of the population is in full-time, paid employment.[23] To an increasing extent, people's lives, interests and identity are focused on relations outside the workplace. More specifically, they are focused on the home, with self-provisioning (DIY, gardening and so forth) representing a sphere of autonomy where they can literally 'be themselves'. Nevertheless, on the basis of his detailed study of households on the Isle of Sheppey, Pahl argues strongly against any romantic vision of deindustrialising but autonomous and happily self-provisioning households.[24] One of his central points is that it is the *already* employed and relatively well-off households who are in fact engaging in such self-servicing. The reason is that they are the people most able to afford the necessary tools and equipment. Moreover, those who do not own their homes have much fewer incentives to become 'do-it-yourselfers'.

A related argument comes from Saunders. At the end of the second edition of *Social Theory and the Urban Question* he argues that to focus on consumption is to focus on an area of social life where individuals can gain maximum control over their lives.

In focusing on that sphere of life which provides the greatest potential for the expression of individual autonomy, urban sociology is uniquely equipped to chart a path out of the 'iron cage' which Weber believed was encompassing the whole of modern society. In the problem of consumption, therefore, urban sociology has not only at long last discovered an object of analysis; it has helped identify one of the core questions of the modern age.[25]

But it is again the home to which Saunders gives his prime attention. In some respects his work echoes that of Dunleavy and Castells. He argues on the basis of his recent survey of working class home owners that ownership does indeed influence political alignments, especially within the middle classes.[26] Unlike Dunleavy, however, he is saying that any 'conservatising' effect of home ownership is a result of the real economic interests people have in the economic value of their properties. Home ownership does not itself have an *embourgoisement* effect.

Of crucial interests to our concerns is a rather more general aspect of Saunders's work on the significance of the home. He believes that the home has a central role in people's consciousness, and specifically in their sense of 'ontological security'. As we have seen, this refers to a sense of knowing who or where you are in a society which has increasingly 'spread' over time and space. Saunders argues that the home has a key role in providing such ontological security, a sense of refuge to which people can retreat and be themselves. And, as people get older, they tend to attach greater significance to the home in providing such security. Furthermore, home *ownership* is a key way in which people obtain such security. Those in public and privately rented housing do not obtain the same sense of personal identity.

Another way of putting this is that the home is an 'escape attempt': a sphere of autonomy to which people can retreat. Such a process has been taking place for a long time. The home can, therefore, be seen as a potentially significant source of ontological security, even if large numbers of people finding such security in the same place at the same time can itself lead to much anxiety.[27]

There is, however, a major counter-argument here alluded to by Saunders. Pahl, Saunders, and indeed Marx, all argued that the home and civil society is a sphere of relative freedom and autonomy compared to the sphere of employment. The question is, however, whether or not this is a peculiarly male vision. Many feminists, by contrast, see the home as predominantly a back region for a man returning home from work: one where he can be himself, and largely at the expense of women's autonomy and escape. The argument goes that it is women who are in fact doing all the reproducing of labour power and servicing other people's escapes. The home is, according to this perspective, therefore, one of the principal sources of gender domination and exploitation.

The home as an escape attempt

Saunders, however, challenges this argument. Following his survey of relatively low-income home owners, he argues that the domestic division of labour within homes is indeed 'strongly patterned by gender, with child care (where relevant), laundry and house cleaning being strongly associated with women while gardening and looking after the car tend to be predominantly male activities'. But he also argues that this should not be seen as automatically implying drudgery and oppression for women. Women are more likely to exercise control over the household budget. Furthermore, women are not tied to the kitchen sink in the way often caricatured by feminist writers. Roughly the same proportion of women and men regularly go out of their homes on a social basis. Perhaps even more significantly, '56 per cent of women and 57 per cent of men said they had no desire to go out any more than they already do'.

Women and men in this group carry out different tasks within the home and they pursue different leisure pursuits (men, for example, are more likely to be tinkering with the car or engaging in DIY). But Saunders argues that it is wrong for feminists to draw from this the idea that home is a place of relaxation for men or a setting for the systematic exploitation of women. For both genders the home is associated first and foremost with a range of deep-lying instincts; those of family, children, love and affection. As a home-owning woman with a skilled manual job puts it:

To feel at home – you never call it your house, it's your home. It's the way you build it up and the people who live in it. . . . It's the house you build together. A house isn't just bricks and mortar, it's the love that's in it.

Similarly, a male manager said:

Your home is with your family. And the things you put into it. You put part of yourself into your housing, don't you?

The second most important association people have with the home is one of relaxation and comfort. Again, this is a feeling shared equally by men and women. A retired male semi-skilled home owner said:

I can dress how I like and do what I like. The kids always brought home who they liked. It's not like other people's places where you have to take your shoes off when you go in.

And a female manager said that:

It's not having everything regimental. Not feeling it's got to be like a furniture showroom to be comfortable. . . . It always annoys me on building sites when it says, 'Wimpey Homes'. They're not homes, they're houses. Home is happiness and family, that sort of thing.

Women and men both, therefore, seem to have very positive feelings about their homes. Saunders makes the important point that these feelings about the home increase as people get older. The implications are that, in a way similar to the class analyses we discussed in the last chapter, there is a major discrepancy between the ways in which social scientists conceptualise what is taking place and how people feel and understand what is taking place. Of course, it is always possible to say that people are suffering from false consciousness (women, for example, are continually suffering from the illusion that they are not being exploited in the home) but that is surely too patronising a view to be taken at all seriously.

The implications are, firstly, that civil society at whatever scale (the 'community' scale as represented by Castells's studies or the scale of the home as represented by Pahl and Saunders) is for many people a setting within which a degree of identity can indeed emerge, albeit in complex and highly diverse ways. But, secondly, a sociology of civil society needs to take far more seriously people's own understandings and self-conceptions. This brings us back to our central theme.

Such understandings and self-conceptions can only be properly appreciated by combining those aspects of social theory which incorporate concepts of class, state, gender or ethnicity with the understandings offered by biology and psychology. An extreme sociobiologist or ethologist might well argue that the fact that women largely enjoy home life is a result of their genetic inheritance. They would probably suggest that during millions of years' evolution, women's instincts have developed in such a way as to protect and nourish family and kin. But this kind of determinism (one denying the mediating social role of culture) is just as misleading as the kind offered by feminists or Marxists. The fact is (however complex and messy the eventual analysis may be) that the two kinds of process and relationship must have developed together and must surely be combined with one another in our understanding.

Saunders's work offers an example of how such a combination might be effected. In the British case (and Saunders makes it clear that he is generalising about the home in British society) the best way in which the occupant of a house can acquire ontological security is through being its owner. Owner-occupation, in other words, offers the greatest opportunities for the management of self. This need not, however, suggest (as Saunders sometimes does indeed imply) that owner-occupation is at all times and in all places an optimum means of gaining control over one's own life.

Pahl's and Saunders's work begins, therefore, to explore the particular emotional and expressive significance of the home. They have broken the mould of the old structuralist and determinist urban sociology. It remains, however, to place their work within a systematic and more general framework. This can be achieved by once more turning to the conceptual framework we have borrowed from Harré *et al.* and again linking our concerns to the broader structures affecting people's lives and social-cum-spatial mobility.

While much existing work on the home concentrates on the social relations and processes affecting people and households, few studies have examined how these broad constraints and relationships shape people's lives, biographies or life courses.[28] There are, however, important exceptions, and they clearly suggest that a first stage must be to see people's housing experience in relation to the whole of their lives, in particular their lives in employment. This comes through very clearly in, for example, Forrest and Murie's study of senior white collar executives and their families.[29] They suggest that these people are indeed highly mobile, largely as a result of the decisions made on their behalf by the large companies and bureaucracies for which they work.

A similar insistence on incorporating an understanding of the constraints and limitations of the labour market as well as those of the housing market comes from Barlow.[30] His work implies that there is a typical 'housing history'; at least for relatively well-off people in contemporary Britain. It is one in which young people often start life in improved or 'gentrified' housing in inner urban areas, thence progressing to large family homes in the outer suburbs and later retiring to a house purpose-made for well-off home owners. All such changes are related not only to people's work lives but to the decisions of (often multinational) house building companies; the latter increasingly investing in 'up-market' houses and retirement homes for people who have seen the value of their home rapidly increase.

These studies nevertheless tend still to treat individuals and households as people 'to whom things happen'. To a large extent, of course, housing careers may indeed be enforced or constrained by market processes or government authorities. But, at the same time, the town chosen or the house actually lived in are still selected by the households themselves. The house, its form and its location, is a commodity providing real options as to how some people, at least, choose to live. Such a choice is made on the basis of how individuals see themselves and wish to be seen by others, and it is possible to conceptualise a characteristic or typical 'moral housing career'. It is one, certainly, shaped by land markets, builders, financiers and the like, but also one resulting from households and individuals seeking status, respect and security.

So the prevailing 'political economy' perspective again needs combining, this time with an emphasis on the expressive order of the home. Clearly the two are closely related: the archetypal Tudorbethan mansion built by a multinational house construction company being, for example, packaged in such a way as to appeal to a middle class household. As Zukin shows in her excellent study of the conversion of old New York factory buildings into up-market flats, deindustrialisation, the flow of capital into property and the rapid emergence of a status-seeking middle class all combine with each other in the New York version of gentrification.[31]

But we can be rather more rigorous about the form of 'moral housing careers' for different social groups. The following two case studies show how the expressive form of the home extends to different types of household.

Housing careers, moral careers and the expressive order of the home

Much of our discussion of the expressive order has concentrated on language and symbols in the form of conversation. But the artefacts, furniture, decor and design also represent a kind of language people use both to express their 'selves' and to communicate with others. A now quite old study by Laumann and House of middle class homes in Detroit shows how this kind of language is used in the making of personal and social identities.[32]

They see the living room and its furnishings as a 'front', one way in which individuals and families could both express themselves as individuals and yet still present themselves as part of a social group. Their study showed that the Anglo Saxon groups who were already well established in the area (and whose parents came from similar backgrounds) indulged in French and Traditional American furniture and ornate wall mirrors. By contrast, the upwardly mobile middle class who had recently 'made it' celebrated their arrival through the conspicuous forms of chic modern decor, including abstract paintings, modern furniture and sculpture and the pared-down aesthetic of the modern movement.

In adopting this chic mode of expression, the *nouveau riche* was effectively distinguishing itself from the traditional middle classes while at the same time flaunting the fact that it had connoisseurship and taste. However, there was (at least in 1960s Detroit) a rub here for the *nouveaux riches*. While they were emulating the design preferred by avant-garde design-professionals, other lower-status social groups were leaving them socially stranded by copying the styles and artefacts of the traditional elites.

Clearly, the homes and household objects that people adopt for purposes of personal and social identity frequently change their nature. Once an elite has established itself, it may well find itself being emulated or used as a reference group by 'lower' social classes. On the other hand, rapidly emerging elites often pride themselves as ahead-of-the-game, a kind of cultural avant-garde. As Laumann and House suggest, they can usually be depended on to adopt design-languages distinguishing themselves from those who have not yet arrived. Perhaps the upwardly mobile middle classes in 1990s Detroit are now surrounding themselves with *post*modern houses and artefacts!

A similar set of ideas and themes can be taken from Rainwater's examination of lower class home life in the massive Pruitt-Igoe public housing projects of St Louis.[33] Analysing tenants' own accounts of their living conditions, he again argues that 'home' and what we have earlier called 'ontological security' actually mean quite different things for different classes. The connotations are also quite different according to gender and property relations.

The home's most basic function is the provision of shelter from the social and physical environment. So, perhaps unsurprisingly, it is this aspect of the home and the security it provides which is of central importance to the poor. As Rainwater put it: 'because the house is a refuge from noxious elements in the outside world, it serves people as a locale where they can regroup their energies for interaction with that outside world'.[34] So, for the very poor the home is primarily a means by which those largely cut off from the rest of society can shelter from further threats and attacks. According to Rainwater, this aspect of 'home' is of particular importance to women.

If 'home' means, though, the defence of self and close kin for what Rainwater calls the 'lower class', it means something quite different for those who have managed to escape from this class and who have achieved a degree of economic and emotional stability. For what Rainwater calls the 'traditional working class' general improvements to the home still have a fairly low priority. People are saving their resources for other basic needs. Questions of 'taste' hardly enter in. On the other hand, this class does concentrate on possessing minimal amounts of equipment and having 'respectable' neighbours. As Rainwater puts it:

This traditional working class is likely to want to economise on housing in order to have money available to pursue other interests and needs. There will be efforts at the maintenance of the house or apartment, but not much interest in improvement of housing level. Families in this group tend to acquire a good many of the major appliances, to centre their social life in the kitchen, to be relatively unconcerned with adding taste in furnishings to comfort. With respect to the immediate outside world the main emphasis is on a concern with the availability of a satisfying peer group life, with having neighbours who are similar, and with maintaining an easy access back and forth among people who are very well known.[35]

But, as the battle for emotional security and economic prosperity starts to be won, questions of self-expression, esteem and self-realisation begin to replace mere self-defence. At this stage expression turns both to the outside or 'front' of the house as well as the internal setting. In fact, both inside and outside are fronts, with individuals and their families as they become better off constructing what Rainwater calls the 'all-American leisure style'. To quote Rainwater again:

Along with the acquisition of a home and yard goes an elaboration of the inside of the house in such a way as not only to further develop the idea of a pleasant and cozy home, but also to add new elements, with emphasis on having a nicely decorated room or family room, a home which closely approximates a standard of all-American affluence.

At this stage the precise form of the household's relation to its property is of critical importance. For, clearly, owner-occupation assists towards these personal and social ends. People who own a property have more freedom to engage in the 'all-American leisure style' if their house belongs to them and not to a public or private landlord.

CONCLUSION: CIVIL SOCIETY AND THE EXPRESSIVE ORDER

This chapter pursues our general theme of exploring locales and localities as the context of interaction between people and the understandings people gain through such interaction. Social and spatial relations both constrain and enable these interactions and understandings. Moral careers are being fought out; property and spatial relations being used as means to these ends. Property and other social relations are both enabling and constraining people's instincts to be self-determined and to protect self and kin.

We addressed civil society in particular; an area of social life currently at the centre of urban sociology, but one which so far incorporates insufficient understanding of human agency. The conceptual framework developed in Chapter 1 shows how such an understanding would allow us systematically to understand civil society as perceived and appreciated by persons engaged in it.

It emerges that civil society provides quite extensive opportunities for self-realisation and autonomy in the context of what Giddens calls the 'time–space distantiation' of social life. These opportunities are much less apparent at the place of work. Nevertheless, the prospects of escape vary considerably by class. This chapter indicates, too, that it may be profitable to re-examine old and currently unfashionable case studies. An example is the 'community studies' tradition of the 1960s.[36] Their special emphasis on family and kin (at the expense of class) is now frequently lampooned. But one of this chapter's implications is that their preoccupations may not have been so misplaced after all.

NOTES AND REFERENCES

1. For Castells's early critique of urban sociology see *The Urban Question*, Arnold, London (1977), and his essay 'Is there an urban sociology?' in C. Pickvance (ed.), *Urban Sociology: Critical Essays*, Tavistock, London, 1976.
2. M. Castells (1983) *The City and the Grassroots*, Arnold, London.
3. See, for example, M. Castells (ed.) (1987) *High Technology, Space and Society*, Sage, Beverly Hills.
4. See P. Dunleavy (1979) 'The urban bases of political alignment', *British Journal of Political Science*, 9, 409–43.
5. J. Baudrillard (1988) *America*, Verso, London. See also 'The ecstasy of communication' in H. Foster (ed.), *Postmodern Culture*, Pluto, London, 1984.
6. J. Baudrillard (1988) ibid., pp. 33–4.
7. J. Lyotard (1984) *The Postmodern Condition*, Manchester University Press, Manchester; F. Jameson (1984) 'Postmodernism, or the cultural logic of late capitalism', *New Left Review*, 146: 53–92; M. Davis (1985) 'Urban

renaissance and the spirit of postmodernism', *New Left Review*, **151**: 106–114; D. Harvey (1989) 'Flexible accumulation through urbanization: reflections on "post-modernism" in the American city' in *The Urban Experience*, Blackwell, Oxford; D. Harvey (1989) *The Condition of Postmodernity*, Blackwell, Oxford; chapter 9 of S. Lash and J. Urry (1987) *The End of Organized Capitalism*, Polity, Oxford.

8. Perhaps surprisingly, bearing in mind that postmodernism has been subjected almost wholly to class analysis, little emphasis has been given to the fact that this form of culture is subject to intense struggle and contest. One way of seeing postmodernism is as a 'packaged up' popular culture, one appropriated from the ways of life led by subordinate populations but cleaned up and dusted down in a form suitable for consumption by the middle classes or 'service class'.

It is unusual to see this process actually taking place, but it is very clear in R. Venturi (1972) *Learning From Las Vegas*, MIT Press. The author starts with a presentation of the gaudy and highly commercialised 'strip' of Las Vegas; the glitzy and popular centre featuring Caesar's Palace (complete with concrete Roman centurions) and much despised by the mainstream architectural profession. By the end of the book, however, these forms (with all their pastiche and historical reference) have found their way back into the language of professional architecture, a language which is eventually designed by, and for, social elites. Postmodernism, as Tom Woolfe puts it in *From Bauhaus to Our House* (Abacus, London, 1983) has the effect of 'coralling' popular culture back into the realm of elite and professionalised dominant culture.

Taking this insight still further, the label 'postmodernism' is itself largely a product of radical academics and commentators who find themselves increasingly alienated and separated from contemporary cultural change and lack of sustained economic and political support. Postmodernism, taking this view, is not an especially useful explanatory device. It is more a commentary on the disenchantment of rogue intellectuals who nevertheless need (in the interest of promoting self, personal esteem and moral careers) to categorise the society from which they are becoming separated even though it also refers to ways of life being led by some factions of the middle classes. See Z. Bauman (1988) 'Is there a postmodern sociology?', *Theory, Culture and Society*, 5: 217–37.

9. J. Goldthorpe, C. Llewellyn and C. Payne (1987) *Social Mobility and Class Structure in Modern Britain* (2nd edn), Oxford University Press, Oxford.

10. P. Bourdieu (1986) *Distinctions*, Routledge, London. J. Goldthorpe *et al.* (1987) op. cit., p. 367.

11. P. Pfeil (1988) 'Postmodernism as a "structure of feeling" ' in C. Nelson and L. Grossberg (eds), *Marxism and the Interpretation of Culture*, Macmillan, London.

12. I. Yablonsky (1962) *The Violent Gang*, Macmillan, London.

13. Of course, Marxist explanations of crime did not start with contemporary deviancy theory. See, for example, F. Engels (1969) *The Condition of the Working Class in England*, Panther, London.

14. See T. Chapman and J. Cook (1988) 'Marginality, youth and government policy in the 1980s', *Critical Social Policy*, **22**.

15. S. Cohen (1987) *Folk Devils and Moral Panics*, Blackwell, Oxford; D. Hebdidge (1979) *Subculture, the Meaning of Style*, Methuen, London.

16. K. Lorenz (1966) *On Aggression*, Methuen, London; R. Ardrey (1967) *The Territorial Imperative*, Collins, London.

17. L. Tiger and R. Fox (1972) *The Imperial Animal*, Secker & Warburg, London.

18. C. Badcock (1986) *The Problem of Altruism*, Blackwell, Oxford.

19. P. Marsh, E. Rosser and R. Harré (1980) *The Rules of Disorder*, Routledge, London.

20. P. Marsh *et al.* (1980) ibid., p. 129.

21. P. Marsh *et al.* (1980) ibid., p. 64.

22. P. Willis (1977) *Learning to Labour*, Gower, Aldershot.

23. R. Pahl (1984) *Divisions of Labour*, Blackwell, Oxford.

24. On self-servicing see, for example, J. Gershuny (1978) *After Industrial Society*, Macmillan, London.

25. P. Saunders (1986) *Social Theory and the Urban Question* (2nd edn), Hutchinson, London, p. 351.

26. P. Saunders (1989) 'The constitution of the home in contemporary English culture', *Housing Studies*, **4**: 3.

27. See D. Hardy and C. Ward (1984) 'Mass escape 1: the non-plan plot', *Architects Journal*, 19 and 26 Dec. See also their *Arcadia for All: The Legacy of a Makeshift Landscape*, Mansell, London, 1984.

28. For the more conventional 'political economy' perspective on housing and the home see, for example, M. Ball (1983) *Housing Policy and Economic Power*, Methuen, London, and P. Dickens, S. Duncan, M. Goodwin and F. Gray (1985) *Housing, States and Localities*, Methuen, London.

29. R. Forrest and A. Murie (1987) 'The affluent homeowner: labour-market position and the shaping of housing histories', in N. Thrift and P. Williams (eds), *Class and Space*, Routledge, London.

30. J. Barlow (1986) 'Economic restructuring and housing provision in Britain', University of Sussex Working Paper in Urban and Regional Studies, no. 54.

31. S. Zukin (1982) *Loft Living. Culture and Capital in Urban Change*, John Hopkins, London. (2nd edn published by Radius, 1987.)

32. E. Laumann and J. House (1970) 'Living room styles and social attributes: the patterning of material attributes in a modern urban community', in E. Laumann, P. Siegel and R. Hodge (eds), *The Logic of Social Hierarchies*, Markham, Chicago.

33. L. Rainwater (1966) 'Fear and house-as-haven in the lower class', *American Institute of Planners Journal*, **32**: 23–31.
34. L. Rainwater (1966) ibid., p. 23.
35. L. Rainwater (1966) ibid., p. 25.
36. It is fair to say, however, that the community studies tradition has found a recent revival with a series of locality studies sponsored by the Economic and Social Research Council: see P. Cooke (ed.) (1989) *Localities*, Unwin Hyman, London. As regards the older community studies, the classic case is, of course, M. Young and P. Willmott (1957) *Family and Kinship in East London*, Routledge, London. More recent are the anthropologically-based studies of home life by, for example, Sandra Wallman. In *Eight London Households* (Tavistock, London, 1988) she insists on seeing low income households as not just simply living off their quite meagre economic resources. Central parts of home life are, she argues, relations to kin and those with households from similar social and ethnic backgrounds.

5

SOCIETY, EMOTIONS AND THE NATION STATE

How should we understand the state, its relationships both to society and to individuals? Why should the national level of the state continue to have such significance to people's politics despite its apparent remoteness from their everyday lives? How do we explain the growth of nationalism, and ethnic claims for autonomy and self-determination, not least those currently taking place within the Soviet Union?

As Smith points out, 'ethnic ties and national loyalties have become more deep rooted than ever'.[1] The postwar period has seen a great rise in ethnicity; starting in the 1950s with areas peripheral to France and Spain and continuing in the 1960s with Britain's 'Celtic Fringe'. The 1980s have seen ethnicity and nationalism escalating in scope; not only within the Soviet Union but in Eastern Europe and a wide range of Third World societies. But we have little understanding of why this should be. Our emphasis on human nature outlined at the beginning of this study provides a large part of the answer.

This chapter is organised as follows. Firstly it discusses the Marxian and Weberian concepts which now provide the basis for urban and regional sociology examining the state and its relations to people. These concepts emphasise class, crisis management and bureaucracy. With some exceptions, however, they have disappointingly little to say about the detailed relationships between people and state, how these are implemented by governments and interpreted by individuals. Nevertheless, we will extract from this work those elements that connect to our concern with the stretching of social systems and its impacts on individuals and social groups.

Basing our work on Giddens, Foucault and the theories of human nature outlined in Chapters 1 and 2, we will be advancing a new perspective, one involving a fundamental contradiction. On the one hand, national and supra-national states attempt to regulate social relations and the relations between individuals (and such regulation leads to tensions and conflicts as classes and individuals try to reassert their personal and collective identities through local state institutions). On the other hand, the state and its leaders also form an important means by which people understand their own circumstances. States' and governments' emphases on nationalism and blood ties has a deep-rooted emotional significance for individuals. We conclude by illustrating these themes with reference to German politics in the 1930s and British politics in the 1980s.

EVERYDAY LIFE AND THE STATE: ESTABLISHED APPROACHES

State theory is, of course, an exceptionally large topic and there have been a number of wide-ranging surveys of the field.[2] Urban politics itself is also a substantial subject and it too has received wide-ranging and systematic attention.[3] Two particular approaches will be distinguished here. Those stemming from Marxism which emphasise the social relations managed by states, and those stemming from Weber which emphasise the role of bureaucratic elites. We will find that they both provide substantial insights into our central theme. They also contain problems. Some of these are simply internal inconsistencies. But they are also extremely limited in terms of our particular interests. They have an inadequate conceptualisation of the relations between states and people and of the emotional significance of nation states.

Marxism, uneven development and citizenship

We have discussed earlier Castells's redefinition of the 'urban' as a concern with collective consumption. He envisaged modern states as becoming increasingly embroiled in the reproduction of a fit and healthy workforce; a service which capitalist enterprises needed but was itself unable or unwilling to undertake.

In some respects, Castells's ideas were a continuation of Marx's and Engels's early ideas.[4] They argued that one role of the state in capitalist society is to save capital from itself. Factory owners pursue their own interests, competing with one another. One outcome was the intense exploitation of labour-forces, ultimately leading to the destruction of the resource on which they were dependent: labour power. Early state intervention over factory hours, therefore, can be seen as public control necessitated by the blind self-destructiveness of capital itself. Such intervention was needed to restore productivity and profitability. To undertake such intervention, governments needed a degree of independence or autonomy from any particular branch or fraction of capital. In a similar way, the state's provision of collective resources can be seen as ensuring a key commodity for competitive and anarchic capitalist societies; that of a refreshed and productive workforce.

Perhaps the main difference between Castells's approach and that of Marx and Engels (and a difference we can use in our new formulation) is that Castells placed much greater emphasis on the fact that state intervention to provide collective resources did not *only* operate in the interests of the capital. It was also a product of people's actions. Urban social movements in the 1960s and 1970s were being organised around demands for such provision, clearly implying that facilities such as decent housing and welfare resources benefit the working class as well as capital.

Contemporary Marxist urban sociology places much less emphasis on the supposed necessity for the state to be engaged in collective consumption. This, of course, reflects recent social change. 'Recommodification' or privatisation in many fields of collective consumption (such as, for example, public sector housing provision) has clearly proved state intervention to be not 'necessary' for successful capital accumulation. Marxist urban politics is now much more coy about all-embracing grand, theoretical claims. Its prime starting-point is that of uneven development of class relations. It is this uneven development that links to our central interest in time–space distantiation and its effects on people's consciousness and actions. Tensions between local and national (or national and supra-national) governments are the political expression of ontological insecurity and the attempt to gain a degree of self-determination.

Uneven development implies, of course, that class relations take quite distinct forms in, say, the USA, Britain, Sweden or Japan. These differences are partly a result of how people have forced governments to introduce legislation. In Sweden, for example, the trade unions have long been well represented in government decision-making and have negotiated pay levels and labour practices much envied by their counterparts in other countries.

Furthermore, class relations take distinct forms within societies. These can again be seen as a result of different social alliances forcing their own interests on to the local political agenda and using the state apparatus towards their own ends. In some regions within a particular society the working class may be exceptionally well organised and trade unionised. In Britain, for example, Merseyside, Sheffield and Glasgow have long been considered to be 'red islands' within British society: the labour movement having forced out of the state substantial levels of collective housing and welfare provision. Meanwhile, red islands in other places such as South Wales have forced state intervention in the form of major industrial investments.[5]

For all these variations, however, there persists in many localities a 'neighbourhood effect' whereby working class people appear consistently drawn towards the politics of the middle classes and employers of their area. The reasons for this have been widely discussed yet remain relatively obscure.[6] One reason may well be that people living in the same locality share, whatever their class position, similar material positions. A working class individual and a middle class individual may have similar political demands when it comes to, say, local educational and welfare facilities, local job opportunities and protection of house prices. In other words, their alliances may be simply the produce of shared material circumstances. We might at this stage, however, recall from Chapter 2 the processes outlined by the Chicago School and, in particular, by G. H. Mead. The 'neighbourhood effect' could also be explained as the product of repeated association between the different classes in the same locality. Mead, it will be recalled, emphasised the role of what he called the 'generalised other' in the making of individuals' values. People, he argued, evaluate themselves by viewing themselves through the eyes of others. The neighbourhood effect could also be understood as the middle classes acting as a 'generalized other' for the working classes of their locality; in effect a reference group, for subordinate social groups, influencing the extent to which they either resist or abide by dominant, and often centralising, political authority.

The neighbourhood effect apart, contemporary urban sociology (especially that deriving from Marxism) envisages local variations in politics and forms of state intervention as straightforwardly the product of the particular balance of class relations constituting a particular locality. Understanding the actual forms and extents of state intervention thereby becomes a largely empirical matter. In the British case, forms and levels of national intervention are seen as closely allied to the particular class interests for which the state is responsible: 'the City' or financial capital (for example, industrial capital) or the trade unions. Forms of government intervention in other societies are seen by Marxists as reflecting varying degrees of class forces. In many societies, for example, manufacturing capital is more influential than it is in Britain.

Furthermore, within nations, local governments and their intervention are seen as largely reflecting the demands made by class interests at the local level. These often tend to include small, 'petit bourgeois' interests. Nevertheless, these reflections of local interests and relationships are, particularly in Britain, being increasingly overseen and overruled by central government.

The emphasis on locality and variable demands on national government is one which we need to retain for our alternative view of the state. But, for all its growing sensitivity to spatial variation, historical change and human agency, Marxist state theory itself remains unevenly developed when it comes to appreciating the links between state and people and the emotional significance of the state. Marx himself did, however, leave some basic clues as to how we might achieve this kind of understanding of the state.[7]

Marx argued that the state and its forms of intervention not only reflect the balance of class relations in capitalist society but atomise, and therefore diffuse (and defuse), imminent class conflict. This is the result of the particular kind of social relationship or 'state form' created by states. 'State form' refers to the fact that states themselves constitute a special form of social relation. People are treated by government-controlled apparatuses as individualised and equal citizens (with distinct legal, electoral and civic rights) rather than members of a class or some other kind of collective group.

One of Marx's key points was, therefore, the individualism inculcated by the state. This theme has gone largely unrecognised by contemporary social theory, including urban and regional sociology. Yet it is a key link in our new emphasis. It means that any individual, including the least powerful, is an equal citizen. Her or his rights before the law are, for example, deemed to be equal to those of a company director. Quite apart from whether this is true in practice, contemporary Marxists have tended to overlook this insight. Or if it is recognised, such individual rights are quickly dismissed as 'bourgeois': freedoms within an otherwise oppressive system of exploitation. Marx's emphasis on how the individual is treated

by the state remains, however, an important one and we will return to it
shortly.

Leaving this central issue to one side for the moment, we should add
here that there are major critiques which can be made of Marxist theories,
critiques on the theories' own terms. The first concerns the continuing
insistence that class and class-based processes are necessarily the principal
mechanisms underlying uneven development and social change. The
questions are, first: What about civil society? As suggested in Chapter 4,
this may be increasingly significant in terms of people's consciousness and
politics.

Secondly: What about kinds of social relation (especially those of
gender and race) and their *combination* with class?[8] Any attempt to
appreciate the political significance of uneven development must surely
undertake the study of the complex interactions between different kinds
of social relations in different localities. Again, an adequate appreciation
of people's understandings and political alignments must surely be rooted
in the whole of their experience and not just that of the workplace.

Still more important from our viewpoint is how the state apparatus
relates to its citizens. It is extremely rare for Marxian analysis to explore
this matter, but Marx's original insight that the state treats people as
separate persons rather than as parts of larger social collectives, has
actually been used and developed by one branch of Marxist state theory.
This approach emphasises the 'state form'.[9] Like most Marxist analyses,
this approach still envisages the state as 'capitalist': an apparatus caught
up in and managing the social relations of capitalism. It recognises,
however, that the way in which this is achieved and experienced is
precisely in the individualised form which Marx recognised.

To this extent, then, a 'state form' analysis does indeed bring welcome
attention to people's experience of the state, especially those people who
are particularly dependent on the resources represented by the state.
Presented below, for example, is a woman interviewed by the London
Edinburgh Weekend Return Group, a group of authors working within
this perspective and insisting on seeing the state as consumers and
producers themselves see it.[10] The woman talking has raised a large family
and needs state resources as her basic income. The key point about her is
that although she obviously needs the state and its resources, she does not
need these in the oppressive, bureaucratic and regulatory forms in which
they come. Here she is assessing the likely outcome of a confrontation
with her local council.

It doesn't get you anywhere. You don't win. They have the majority every time. You can go down to the council and rant and rave, you still won't get anything. If you go down and ask in a polite way, then you might get what you want. (p. 13)

So, unsurprisingly, she ensures that she does nothing to cross the 'important' people on which she is dependent.

They are important to me these people. I do have to depend on them. I can't afford to take risks. (p. 14)

Indeed, she believes that she is caught up in a bureaucratic cage, the different branches of the council being in league with local and national branches of other sections of the state apparatus. Paranoia creeps in.

If you get into trouble with one, the other is likely to know. That is what I think, anyway. (p. 15)

This woman's understanding of local government is, incidentally, a useful commentary on the idea that local governments and state organisations are somehow especially responsive to people's everyday lives. She sees the state, in its local manifestation at least, as a faceless, alien and still distant bureaucracy. Indeed, regular contact with the state only reinforces this view.

Bureaucracy, corporatism and the nation

The above extracts, although used by Marxist authors, in fact also reflect a Weberian perspective on the state. A Weberian approach emphasises the effects on people's life-chances of bureaucracy. The emphasis, therefore, shifts away from the uneven development of class relations and towards elites within the state apparatus, seeing them as the key, relatively autonomous decision-makers.

Weber's approach to the state was quite distinct from that of the Marxist tradition, although the thrust of our argument will be that it can be usefully combined with this tradition. Marx's followers insist on politics and state intervention being largely a product and reflection of underlying class relations. They give little attention not only to how it is understood and experienced but also to the relations between bureaucracies and elected politicians. Weberians, by contrast, give much attention to the state itself, arguing that it should be seen as a set of social processes relatively independent of class relations.

More specifically, Weber envisaged state bureaucrats as of key importance in creating this autonomy. They have their own values and priorities, not the least of which is their self-preservation and acquisition of social status. Their status and rewards are, like those of many other social groups, achieved through acquiring special forms of expertise. Training and qualifications are therefore needed. The managers argue that these are required in order to guarantee a good service. Weberians argue, however, that expertise is also used to achieve 'social closure'; the insistence on examined skills being means by which scarcity, and hence material rewards, are maintained.

Crucially, from Weber's perspective, the values and actions of state bureaucrats tend to override the policies of elected politicians. Yet the claim of the bureaucrats is that they are working in a dispassionate general, even national, interest; working for the good of all society. British television has mounted a highly successful comedy series called *Yes Minister*, the main theme of which has been an elected cabinet minister being constantly deflected from his preferred politics by senior permanent officials primarily concerned to protect their own positions. Political strategies likely to affect the positions of the bureaucrats themselves are, therefore, systematically obfuscated and dismantled. *Yes Minister* is, therefore, a popular version of one of Weber's main themes: state strategies, and variations in such strategies, being primarily the product of unelected officials working for faceless bureaucracies.

There are a number of ways in which we can link Weberian theory to our particular interests. The first concerns the controllers, or managers, to which Weberians give such emphasis. The 1970s saw some highly productive 'urban' work using a Weberian perspective, Pahl providing the main stimulus for this approach.[11] Detailed empirical work by, for example, Davies and Kramer and Young, focused on the ways in which planners and other public officials managed not only to frustrate the intentions of elected officials but, often in a highly paternalistic way, created strategies which simultaneously operated in their own interests while still deemed to be in the interests of the general public.[12] The work was paralleled by a similar focus on private sector 'gatekeepers': senior managers such as estate agents and landlords again being seen of critical importance in who gets what at the 'urban' level.[13]

However, Pahl later changed his argument to suggest that a myopic focus on bureaucrats themselves was unjustified. Public and private sector managers alike were caught up in wider social systems. As such, they could not be considered as autonomous agents. Rather than simply imposing their own preferences on policies and resource levels, they have critical effects in terms of mediating wider social relations and processes. To put this another way, managers work within larger societies.[14]

This reconsideration of the original managerial thesis was eventually linked to an alternative and wider conceptualisation of the state, state officials and their relation to society. It is at this point that this perspective relates to another of our central themes: that of nationalism and the national interest. The alternative to managerialism was 'corporatism', a concept which had earlier found application in the study of fascism but which was now dusted off for use in what seemed like a new social era.[15] There are a number of different versions of this concept but essentially it argues that capitalist societies are tending towards a set of relationships between social groups and between these groups and the state. Society is envisaged as composed of a series of 'corporations' such as trade unions and businesses; and, as regards politics and public strategy-making, these are represented by elites.

Mediating the differences between these groups and guiding them towards mutually agreed goals is the overriding notion of the national interest. The central purpose is to hammer out long-term strategies for the nation as a whole. Crucially, however, incorporation into the upper reaches of strategy-making is offered only to representatives of the respectable citizenry. It entails responsibilities as well as privileges. Trade union leaders, for example, are expected to regulate their members' demands and to desist from strategies which are not agreed with representatives of business. Similarly, business has to enter into agreements. These might include, for example, a commitment to certain levels of investment, wage levels or even working conditions. A national, unifying interest thereby prevails; even if this results in diminishing the importance of parallel political decision-making in elected parliamentary assemblies.[16]

So Weberian theory has slowly shifted its concerns away from bureaucrats to a related interest in the tendency for state officials to be operating in a corporatist manner: mediating between warring groups in the 'national interest'. As should have become clear, however, the main explanations within this shifting strand of thinking about politics and elites have been conducted primarily in the broad social and economic spheres: little attention has been given to the relations between states and people. This is somewhat surprising given that Weberian sociology gives particular significance to the values, intentions and interpretations which people have of their lives and social relations.

The dominant theme in this perspective, one which we can pick up and develop with our particular perspective, is that of the state as a great power container, operating in a general or national interest but at the same time regulating people's everyday lives.

DAILY LIFE AND THE NATION STATE

We have so far discussed a number of themes in conventional political theory. From Weber and early Marx comes the idea of the state's relationship to individuals. From Weber comes the emphasis on a national or general interest, one represented by state managers and officials. From later Marxists comes the idea that individuals' daily lives are caught up in quite distinct local forms of social relation. We will now develop these themes and combine them in a systematic way to construct an improved understanding of the relationship between daily life and the nation state. This will reflect the themes illustrated in Chapters 1 and 2 and will be illustrated with two studies of working class politics.

A good starting-point for developing an improved understanding of the state are Foucault's and Giddens's recent works.[17] Giddens's approach is indeed partly based on Foucault, but it also draws on Goffman whose studies of 'total institutions' we touched on in Chapter 1. In *Discipline and Punish* Foucault argues that state power and administrative control took a new and distinctive form from the late eighteenth century onwards. His book starts with highly explicit descriptions of horrific torture and physical violence, these being the principal means by which social order was maintained in the earlier era.

The new form of administrative control is, for Foucault, represented by the panopticon, a device designed in the late eighteenth century by the philosopher Jeremy Bentham. Figure 5.1 shows a section through this device. It is a circular building with a large central hall marked E and the prisoners or those under surveillance and regulation in the positions marked H. At the centre is an inspection lantern, a cylinder in which the inspector sits (Figure 5.2). This is made of paper-thin material pierced by a number of small lenses. The result is that the inspector (in Weberian terms, the manager) has total surveillance of the whole institution but without being seen. Meanwhile the separated and isolated prisoners, having no 'back regions' in which to hide, reflect on their sins and eventually emerge as reformed characters. Bentham suggested that the

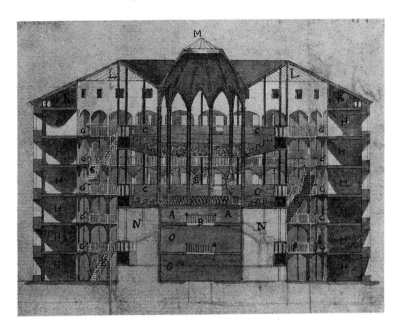

Figure 5.1 The panopticon penitentiary, 1791 (section). (Courtesy of the Library, University College, London, ms. 119a, f. 24.)

device had a range of applications. Besides factories it could be used as a device in which managers could survey workers, or teachers keep a close but invisible eye on their pupils.

Foucault makes a number of general points about the panopticon. It involves the centralisation of power and its concentration in the hands of experts (such as prison governors, teachers, factory managers) with special knowledge. This enabled them, for example, to classify 'deviance' and to separate different types of deviant into distinct forms of institutions or into different sections within institutions. Such knowledge and classification represents subjugation of the rest of the population, and the regularisation and standardisation of moral careers. Spectacular physical violence gives way to silent coercion. Secondly, Foucault argues that the panopticon is much more than a building. It symbolises the emergent way in which social relations are managed; the individualisation, classification and invisible control being the characteristic means by which power is established and maintained in contemporary societies.

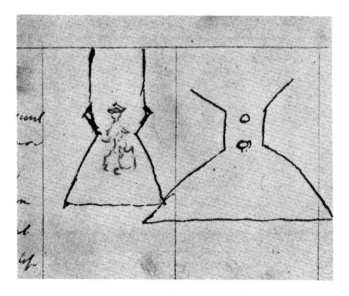

Figure 5.2 Marginal outlines of the inspection lantern from the Bentham Papers. (Courtesy of the Library, University College, London, ms. 119a, f. 24.)

This view of the state is developed by Giddens. He sees surveillance as the 'mobilising of administrative power' with the storage and control of information the key way in which such mobilisation takes place.[18] He therefore gives extended treatment to the new forms of communications, transport and technology which have enabled 'panopticism' to be extended throughout nation states. He also develops Foucault in suggesting that the classification of space (what he calls its 'regionalisation' and 'sequestration') is intimately bound up with these forms of surveillance and control.

Like Weber, Giddens argues that in older 'class-divided' societies (such as those of the Middle Ages), state power largely corresponded with cities themselves. Now, he suggests, it is nation states, not cities, which are 'the most prominent new power-containers'.[19] The sequestration of activities into distinct regions and zones is a key means by which control can be maintained and resources allocated. Locales such as inner cities, suburbs or even regions can be monitored by the authorities as front or back regions.

But Giddens goes beyond Foucault in arguing that this sequestration, as well as enabling the administration of state power, is associated with profound forms of individual and social malaise. These may in turn pose problems as regards the maintenance of social order. At this point Giddens is touching on the deep-lying emotional instincts outlined in Chapters 1 and 2.

He argues that in contemporary society 'routinisation of day-to-day social life is precarious, resting upon a relatively shallow psychological base'.[20] The separation and spatial spread of social life means that people do not regularly encounter the significant experiences of life: birth, sexuality, madness, illness, death and so on. Clearly, being separated from these troubling experiences may well be a benefit, but Giddens is arguing that it also leaves the routines of everyday life relatively empty. It means that individual and social life is lived at a superficial level, leading to 'ontological insecurity' – the separation of the individual from her or his biological and psychological being.

It is at this point that the nation state begins to acquire a psychological as well as a purely administrative significance. Giddens argues that:

The emptiness of the routines followed in large segments of modern social life engender a psychological basis for affiliation to symbols that can both promote solidarity and cause schism. Among these symbols are those associated with nationalism.[21]

As well as being, then, a means of administration and management of social relations, the state, and its symbols of home, land, family, nationhood and communal experience, are also seen as offering a sense of identity and security: especially to people who have little understanding and control over the processes affecting their everyday lives.

Meanwhile Giddens's work requires some comment. He gives, perhaps as a result of a Weberian starting-point to much of his analysis, great attention to bureaucracy and the extent to which populations are very directly monitored and controlled by those with power. This leads him to offer a somewhat partial view of Foucault's important work. One of Foucault's most significant insights is that the controller at the centre of the panopticon does not actually need to be in the lantern for pacification of the surrounding inmates to take place.

Foucault is actually arguing that 'control' need not take place through the direct and constant surveillance of individuals by authorities. Clearly, outright control does indeed take place, but on a day-to-day level social stability is secured largely through people *feeling* that they might be under scrutiny. Foucault is therefore making the subtle and perceptive point that contemporary societies are largely characterised by *self*-policing and introspective control of feelings rather than the explicit display and use of force and authority. This implies that Giddens may be wrong to give such enormous emphasis to the state's directly coercive role.

An example of the application of Foucault to the 'urban' sphere is Dear and Wolch's research on what Giddens would no doubt call the 'sequestrated region' of North American inner cities.[22] They trace the movement of dependents on the state from special enclosed institutions to the 'community' of the inner city. The recipients of welfare concentrated in this highly segregated zone are no doubt subject to the direct surveillance of state officialdom. Inner cities are, after all, back regions for middle class opinion. But Dear and Wolch's main point is that the daily lives of those dependent on welfare are suffused in largely intangible and invisible ways by the institutions on which they are dependent. Their lives, or more precisely their 'moral careers', are certainly regulated by bureaucracy and officialdom, and, eventually, by dominant social interests; but again, the word 'surveillance' overemphasises the degree of detailed, continuing and direct control which any state would find difficult to sustain.

TOWARDS A REVISED UNDERSTANDING: THE STATE AND THE INDIVIDUAL

We have argued for a revised theory of the relations between state and people: one reflecting the role of states in managing social relations and moral careers but one which recognises too that states, in representing a general or 'national' interest, have an important emotional significance. In other words, we are linking the state to the biological and instinctive bases of individual and social life which we insisted earlier should form a part of contemporary urban sociology. It would be easy to dismiss this significance were it not for the fact that general or national interests continue to be important and highly effective rallying cries for much of contemporary politics.

How can we develop this perspective? A first stage is to re-emphasise the individualising and atomising role of states, these representing an important part of Weberian theory and Marx's early speculations on the state. Recent years have seen a developing concern with individualism and the resulting difficulties surrounding working class political organisation.

Olson's early work laid particular emphasis on individual behaviour and motivation. He suggested that people's interests are best served by pursuing personal gains.[23] A member of the working class is more likely to benefit through securing the benefits of collective organisation while doing the least possible to actually create such collectives. In short, instrumentalism (the use of organisation to personal ends or the ends of close kin) is the best tactic for self-advancement. Such an argument finds support in Goldthorpe *et al.*'s empirical study of affluent workers.[24] Their examination of Luton again found that the contemporary working class politics is essentially organised around the support and benefit of self and family. Collective organisations (trade unions, local political parties and so forth) were basically used as means to this end.

Olson's original arguments have been further developed by Offe and Wisenthal.[25] They argue that an important distinction is to be made between the capacities of capital and labour in recognising and acting on their best interests. While it is true that working class politics is highly individualistic and subject to the so-called free rider problem, there are many fewer problems for capital. Whereas working class collective action always faces the difficulty of individualism, self-interest and fragmentation, the collective interests of capital are less ambiguous – simply to make profits. As Savage puts it, 'a hundred shares can be organised and directed more easily than a hundred workers'.[26]

The individualism identified by Olson and others is, however, two-edged. On the one hand, individuals (and working class individuals in particular) may have great difficulty in identifying and pursuing their collective self-interest. This leaves them open to the very 'panopticism' identified by Foucault and Giddens. On the other hand, as also identified by Giddens (and, before him, Freud) there are innate processes leading to a recognition by individuals of the common or national interests represented by the state.

Unfortunately for the Left, however, these are not necessarily collective *working class* organisations. Rather, they are forms of politics and working class organisations which seem best to represent the interests of individuals and close kin. To explore this alternative dimension to politics we must return to Freud who, with LeBon, developed his distinctive theory of politics and the state.

Freud, as suggested in Chapter 2, argued that the state and politics are transferred father figures: organisations and people on whom those with little power and authority can depend for safeguards while at the same time suffering imposed personal restrictions. Similarly, nationalism with its symbols of family, common blood and origins has profound overtones for the individual psyche.[27] 'Homeland' again provides a strong sense of solidarity, collective enterprise, community, kinship and religious ties. And, as Giddens and many earlier social theorists have suggested, time–space distantiation means that these senses of personal and collective identity are a decreasing feature of contemporary social life. This further implies that nationalism and appeals to common blood and homeland are far from being 'old fashioned'. Rather, as people's lives become increasingly disconnected from emotional lives, and from the structures affecting them, they will find increased solace in institutions, individuals and themes associated with apparent, but displaced, notions of kin, blood relations and general or collective experience.

Such explanations of allegiance to the state and to charismatic patriarchal figures are in themselves too vague in this generalised form. They are important in understanding the instincts lying behind people's relations to ethnic, racial and nationalist politics but we need to become much more specific about the social and historical circumstances in which these latent feelings are actually felt and expressed. They need, in short, combining with the social or 'political economy' explanations as represented by the Marxian and Weberian traditions.

Instincts, the individual and the state: The case of the Third Reich

The best way, then, to deal with the complaint that psychological-cum-biological theories of the state are too vague is to attempt a combination between these theories and those we reviewed at the beginning of this chapter. We must again try to understand not only the instinctive bases of people's understanding of politics and the state, but the way in which this is constructed by social relations, including the class relations to which Marxists give such prominence and the relations between governments and people emphasised by Weberians. These connections can only really be understood by looking at concrete historical instances.

There are only a few studies with which we can illustrate this approach. A small amount of work attempting to explain German fascism is an important example. This includes Fromm's study of the industrial working class and the factors determining its support of fascism.[28] Most of his respondents were radically opposed to national socialism, but he established that a generally left-wing outlook amongst his samples was being dissipated by underlying personality traits, in particular their susceptibility to follow father-like authoritarian leaders.

A better-known study from the same period is Reich's *The Mass Psychology of Fascism*, written in the early 1930s.[29] Essentially, Reich was attempting an amalgam of Freudian psychology and Marxism to explain the appeal of Hitler and the rise of fascism. The deepest layer of human nature, he argued, was one in which 'man is essentially an honest, industrious, co-operative, loving and, if motivated, a rationally hating animal'.[30] Reich argued, however, that over thousands of years these essentially good characteristics of humanity had been repressed. Cultures, especially the patriarchal cultures instilled into children in the first four or five years of their lives, had now distorted an essentially benign human nature. Art is one of the few means left of making contact with an essentially 'good' nature. By contrast, fascism, Reich argued, appeals to a thoroughly perverted human nature.

[It is] the basic emotional attitude of the suppressed man of our authoritarian machine civilisation and its mechanistic–mystical conception of life. It is the mechanistic–mystical character of modern man that produces fascist parties, and not vice versa.[31]

Fascism, he argued, made populist appeals to all sections of the community, including large numbers of workers. Indeed, Reich's book was partly a response to the 1932 elections in which the Nazis made large gains amongst the working class. He was also attempting to persuade the Communist Party that they must better understand the primordial needs of the masses: the demand for personal security and sexuality.

The working classes' basic humanity had, Reich argued, been distorted by bourgeois values and priorities. But, more specifically still, he saw fascist mentality as 'the mentality of the little man who is enslaved and craves authority and is at the same time rebellious.'[32] It is at this point that his analysis starts to become much more specific about the particular kind of capitalism with which he was dealing and the especially important group supporting fascism. Who, in class terms, was 'the little man'?

Hitler's Germany saw the resurgence of 'big' or 'monopoly' capital, much of which supported the Fuhrer's war machine. Indeed, Hitler's rise to power was based on a promise to fight on behalf of the powerless against 'big business'. The 'little man' in this particular instance was the little businessman; under constant threat from hyperinflation and threatened with the abyss of unemployment and destitution.

The 'little' businessman was, however, one of the principal supporters of fascism. This was because, Reich argued, it was especially this individual and the family around him which espoused the grand values of nationhood, home and patriarchal authority. In competition with other small businesses, the archetypal 'little man' had clawed his way to success through clinging to such beliefs. He was a boss, not of a firm, but of his own family. He was using the middle classes as a reference group; aspiring to what he believed to be their values of 'honour' and 'duty'. There was, therefore, a special mentality about the small businessman, one quite distinct from that of either the working class or the manager of a large organisation, and one which corresponded with the ideology of a master race. Furthermore, this 'little' businessman even identified with the Fuhrer himself. As Reich puts it:

The reactionary middle-class man perceives *himself* in the Fuhrer, in the authoritarian state. On the basis of this identification he feels himself to be a defender of the 'national heritage' of 'the nation'.[33]

The family unit, and especially the unit as headed by the 'small businessman' was therefore seen by Reich as of critical significance to the rise of fascism. Adding to this was the fact, as they saw it, that potentially revolutionary working class families and heads of household were actually developing petit bourgeois values.

Nor only was it the 'little man' who was particularly prone to sexual repression. More important still for Reich was the fact that his wife and children also suffered from his patriarchal authority. The family and home was a miniature version of the nation state. If the husband is the fuhrer of his family then his wife is the small-scale motherland, the guarantor of future generations. Of course, these generations had, at all costs, to be kept racially clean through the exclusion of non-Aryan blood. For Reich, therefore, the petit bourgeois partriarchal family lay at the heart of fascism. The explanation was simultaneously social, economic and psychological. The solution lay in the abolition of the patriarchal family. As he put it:

Sexually awakened women, affirmed and recognised as such, would mean the complete collapse of the authoritarian ideology.[34]

The 'little man' did not, of course, support German fascism without active encouragement of the Fascist Party. Hitler's politics were deliberately constructed around the fears of the 'little man', their 'little lives' in 'little villages' and the appeal of the nation as giving some sense to this struggle. Indeed, Hitler represented his own life as a prototypical moral career of the little man. Here is Hitler's own account of his model moral career, one to be emulated by his audience.

I have come from the people. In the course of fifteen years I have slowly worked my way up from the people, together with this Movement. No-one has set me above this people. I have grown from the people, I have remained in the people, and to the people I shall return.[35]

As regards the calculated appeal to the frightened little man trying to make sense of his everyday struggle for life in his market town or small village, Hitler continually stressed the nation:

Now that we meet here, we are filled with the wonder of this gathering. Not every one of you can see me and I do not see each of you. But I feel you, and you feel me!

It is faith in our nation that has made us little people great, that has made us poor people rich, that has made us wavering, fearful, timid people brave and confident, that has made us erring wanderers clear-sighted and has brought us together!

So you have come this day from your little villages, your market towns, your cities, from mines and factories, or leaving the plough, to this city. You come out of the little world of your daily struggle for life, and of your struggle for Germany and for our nation, to experience this feeling for once. Now we are together, we are with him and he is with us, and now we are Germany![36]

We have been arguing here for a view of the state in which governments are managing not only class and social relations but also individuals. These individuals may be frightened by and greatly distanced from the power and authority of the state, but in an important sense they also need the state; its appeal to a higher authority as well as its power and resources. The responses by these members of the Frankfurt School of Sociology to Hitler's rise represent the kind of perspective we are looking for. Reich's analysis is in many respects highly persuasive, even if some of his concepts are difficult to accept. He made the connections between the social and instinctive bases of behaviour we have been demanding. He is also dealing with our insistence on historically specific analysis.

On the other hand, Reich is not above criticism. As a dedicated Marxist, he almost certainly makes too many unwarranted assumptions about the supposed 'purity' of basic human nature and its distortion by culture and civilisation. It is arguable, too, that he was over-anxious to dismiss people's attempts to preserve the family as 'ideology', one distracting attention from the class basis of fascism. As we discussed earlier and argue later, this 'ideology' has deep biological and emotional reverberations and cannot be easily dismissed as generated by propaganda or clever oratory.

For all these criticisms, however, Reich's study is perhaps the best empirical example of how politics, and nationally-based politics in particular, is simultaneously the result not only of daily life (and people's attempts to construct an understanding of their particular experience) but also of deep-lying social sexual and psychic structures. It shows, too, how some of the more conventional concepts of urban sociology link to our additional emphasis on human nature. Fascism was the high-point of corporatism. Our argument is that this type of politics has a strong basis in instincts and emotion as well as in political economy.

It is perhaps easy to construct such an understanding in the highly exceptional and extreme circumstances of the rise of fascism. But how can we generalise the argument and extend it to more 'normal' circumstances?

The individual and the state: Developing the argument

It can be argued that Reich's work has much to tell us about contemporary politics. In some ways, however, it seems quite difficult to extend his approach to more 'normal' politics and yet the persistence, and even growth, of nationalism and ethnicity as a basis for politics and social upheaval need some kind of explanation.[37] Here we need to restate and elaborate on our general proposition, this time with the aid of Van den Berghe's work.

One half of our argument is that states (and national states in particular) are indeed conducting the functions outlined by Marxist and Weberian commentators: those of managing the social relations of capitalism and regulating and classifying individual citizens and their activities or moral careers. These are the social functions of contemporary states, even if this perspective overemphasises the oppressive nature of state apparatuses. But authors such as Fromm and Reich are a good reminder of the second half of the argument: that states and leaders are also powerfully attractive to the individuals they are supposedly subjugating. Not only are their resources in demand, but they make powerful appeals to instinct and emotion.

This latter is the common theme associated with the contemporary nationalist and ethnic movements. The central drives are those to which we gave considerable prominence at the start of this book, and are those associated with survival and identity, as well as with the preservation and expansion of family, kin and blood relations. Furthermore, nationalism in all its many forms, is the continuing, and largely unconscious, search for personal identity in societies where relations of blood and kin are being lost.

This loss is a result of what we have earlier seen Giddens calling 'time-space distantiation': the increasing spread of social life over space and time. Ethnic groups have now spread well away from original kin relations. But this does not stop people instinctively protecting themselves and kin substitutes. A way of developing this view is with the work of Van den Berghe.[38] He argues that people in contemporary societies are increasingly obliged to depend on 'markers of ethnicity' as a means of identifying who they are and where they belong. These markers are outward signs portraying whether or not individuals and collections of people belong to the same ethnic group.

In contemporary societies these are necessarily of a cultural or social nature; nationality and territory being crude and highly approximate signifiers of shared ancestry. One such marker (and one to which Van den Berghe gives little attention) is religion. Contemporary political struggles organised on religious lines clearly need social and economic explanations. On the other hand, the enormous power of charismatic patriarchal leaders combined with the assertion of common ancestry or blood are quite explicit parts of such politics. Again, an understanding of biologically and psychologically based emotions helps us understand such social movements, many of which seem irrational and beyond explanation.

'Ethnic markers' are, then, a basic mechanism underlying the politics of nationalism, ethnicity and religion. Yet crucial to Van den Berghe's work, and indeed central to our argument, is that these instinctive drives involved in establishing personal and social identity are only latent. They will take many different forms and indeed they may not be self-evident in the 'real' concrete world at all. They are, in effect, triggered off by very specific and local forms of social relationship and the threats they pose to everyday life. As we have seen, in the Third Reich it was the specific circumstances of the rise of monopoly capital, the corporatist state organised as protecting national purity, hyperinflation, the rapid rise in unemployment and perceived threats to the 'little man'. In the various USSR states seeking autonomy, in Northern Ireland or in Palestine the contingent circumstances are again wholly unique. This despite the fact that the eventual outcomes, nationalism and defence of territory, are quite similar.

Reich's identification of the family with the German fatherland is, therefore, a special case of a more general phenomenon. A particular set of social alliances and historical circumstances led to this specific version of nationalism. The mechanisms underlying nationalism here and elsewhere are therefore those identified by the geneticists and ethologists reviewed earlier: the instincts for expansion and protection of kin. The particular form of nationalism identified by Reich is also quite general: one led by a charismatic leader figure, the figure identified by Freud as the lost father or mother.

Given this conceptual framework, it is surely misleading to dub nationalism as simply 'ideological'. Still less is it a set of con-tricks to which deluded individuals and households continually fall prey. Nationalism is linked to deep-rooted human instincts and cannot be easily ascribed to clever politicians. The causal powers involved are real enough. They are just as real as the class relations to which Marxists give such prominence or to the state bureaucracies which Weberians emphasise. The point can now be clarified by turning to another illustration, one based on a contemporary debate concerning the changing nature of British politics.

Instincts, the individual and the state: The case of contemporary British politics

The debate began with the Marxist commentator, Stuart Hall, attempting to explain the emergence and success of Thatcherism.[39] The difficult problem for him is why those people (especially the working class) who seem to be suffering most from a particular political regime actually support it. Hall used the concept of 'authoritarian populism' as a means of explaining this apparent masochism. Authoritarian populism refers to the ways in which successive Thatcher governments managed to harness and actively use a wide range of popular discontents to form a regime which relied considerably on heavy-handed, Victorian morality and even increased coercion. Hall uses the work of the 1920s' Italian Marxist, Gramsci, to suggest that while new forms of politics are related to economic change and crisis, they cannot simply be 'read off' from such developments. Political strategy is considered to have a dynamism of its own, one not determined by economic change.

'Authoritarian populism' is seen by Hall as the latest stage in a long historical development of postwar British politics. Corporatism as a means of intervention has, at the time of writing, largely broken down. The alliances are primarily between central government and big capital. In any event, the working class feels thoroughly uninvolved in this type of 'national interest' strategy. The breakdown of corporatism, however, left a space for the introduction of New Right strategies. This entailed dropping direct and centrist management and harnessing negative feelings for the state: anti-bureaucracy, anti-collectivism and anti-'creeping socialism'. New Right philosophies, as applied in Britain, also exploited rising popular anxieties about crime and delinquency. This has led, Hall argues, to an increasing 'moral authoritarianism', one involving, for example, the strengthening of the police force, a re-emphasis on family life as a means of controlling juvenile delinquency, increased calls for capital punishment, and a general return to old or 'Victorian' values.

The explanation is, therefore, partly economic: successive governments having consistently failed to create a national consensus around the restoration of a productive national economy. Hall gives special significance, though, to 'popular morality' and the ways in which 'new kinds of commonsense' have been established and imposed in the recent period. Hall uses the Marxist philosopher Althusser and the social psychology of Laclau to argue that politics is not just about individuals and social groups pursuing their immediate material interests; it is also about how they imagine and identify themselves in relation to the wider social world. Similarly, governments address people in these 'imagined' capacities. They are addressed as individuals and families and, furthermore, as *frightened* individuals and families, afraid of being crushed by, say, a socialist bureaucracy or large masses of immigrants.

According to Hall, therefore, authoritarian populism respecifies people's material interests. Thatcherism's long-term aim was the establishment of the 'correct' basic values. These are the values of a supposedly 'lost' British culture; one in slumber but waiting to be awakened. Mrs Thatcher herself is seen as the guardian of these traditional wisdoms. She encapsulates the new commonsense: the housewife managing the nation in a way familiar to the ordinary household (not spending more than it is earning) and bringing home to her striking trade unionised husband the 'harsh realities and consequences of living without a weekly wage'.

Hall's ideas led, however, to a substantial critique by Jessop *et al.*[40] They argued against what they termed Hall's 'ideologism', suggesting that it is too elastic, descriptive and lacking in explanatory content. In his attempt to establish that there is a form of discourse associated with politics which is relatively separate from economic change, Hall is seen as neglecting the 'structural underpinnings of Thatcherism'. These are not just the shifting form of the economy and the rise of financial capital at the expense of productive capital. They are also the continuing decline of parliamentary politics and political control increasingly orchestrated by a small clique within the Cabinet. Britain, according to Jessop *et al.*, is moving towards a presidential system of government.

The concept of authoritarian population implies, for Jessop *et al.*, a monolithic, relatively stable and widely supported form of government. They argue, however, that none of these assumptions is justified. Nevertheless, the government is 'populist' and does indeed rely on the idea of a common national project. It is, however, a project endorsed by 'good citizens' and 'hard workers' and one threatened by a subordinated Second Nation. The latter includes, for example, trade unionists who go on strike or local authorities (such as the abolished Greater London Council) who do not aspire to this kind of populism. So 'ideology' is important for Jessop *et al.*, but it is of a different form from that suggested by Hall. Their central point, though, is that the authoritarianism which Hall identifies stems almost wholly from attempts to manage a political and economic system in crisis.

It seems at first difficult to proceed with this debate. On the one hand, Jessop *et al.* are clearly right to emphasise that new forms of politics and people's support of these politics must be in some way connected to changing social structures and crises within capitalist society. It is precisely such crises which lead to 'escape attempts' in the form of the 'national interest' or placing of faith in charismatic, father or mother figure leaders. On the other hand, this still leaves us searching for explanations as to why authoritarian and highly nationalist strategies should receive such widespread and systematic support. Hall does, indeed, seem to be touching on some very important issues with his insistence on a relatively separate sphere of discourse and communication. The problem is, however, that his Marxist conceptual framework leaves him describing this sphere as 'ideology' or 'hegemony'. It is left unexplained and, furthermore, Jessop *et al.* cannot help him out because they too are caught in the same conceptual framework. For them, too, it is simply ideology and false consciousness.

The clearest way forward is to break out of the restrictive conceptual framework within which both Hall and Jessop *et al.* are trapped while still using their insights regarding the economic or social bases of Thatcherism. The 'authoritarian populism' of the 1980s, the corporatism of the 1960s and 1970s or presumably of some other form of nationalism in the 1990s are simultaneously a product of *both* capitalist social relations *and* the instinctive support which people, especially those least certain of their and their family's future, give to parliaments and their leaders. Again, therefore, we are looking for explanations which combine Marx with the insights of writers such as LeBon and Freud. As regards the latter, Rose has recently adopted a Freudian interpretation of the repeated re-election of Margaret Thatcher, one which seems in line with the framework we are adopting. Rhetorically, she asks:

What if Thatcher was re-elected not despite the repugnance that many feel of her image, but also in some sense because of it? What if that forceful identity for which she is so severely castigated somewhere also operates as a kind of pull?[41]

CONCLUSION: LEARNING FROM THE NEW RIGHT

This chapter, like those before, attempts a fusion of conventional sociological approaches to urban and regional studies with approaches emphasising the emotional and biological bases of social life. We apply such a combination here to an issue which has been of central interest to urban sociology: the state, its concentration of power, and its relation to people's daily lives.

The chapter is another lesson in the value of exploring perspectives which may at first seem wholly incompatible. The psychological theories of political leaders and the state reviewed here have strong echoes in New Right thinking.[42] The latter also emphasise the dependency relations which state intervention forces on people. The alternative, they argue, is to let the great mass of people engage in market processes, freeing themselves from such dependency. State welfare would be used towards this end, providing people with additional disposable income. When interpreted by political leaders and government officials in actual societies, however, the philosophies of the New Right become used as excuses for decreasing levels of welfare altogether. In this way the original insights of New Right thinking have acquired for themselves a bad name.

But if our account of the role of contemporary states is correct, it suggests that the original New Right philosophies on the importance of the state to individuals and families may still have much to offer. Perhaps they are at least 'Half Right'.

NOTES AND REFERENCES

1. A. Smith (1987) *The Ethnic Revival*, Cambridge University Press, Cambridge, p. 1.

2. See, for example, P. Dunleavy and B. O'Leary (1987) *Theories of the State*, Macmillan, London.

3. See, for example, P. Dunleavy (1980) *Urban Political Analysis*, Macmillan, London.

4. See, for example, F. Engels (1884) *The Origin of the Family, the State and Private Property*, reprinted in *Selected Works* (1958), Lawrence & Wishart, London.

5. On 'red islands' see, for example, P. Dickens, S. Duncan, M. Goodwin and F. Gray (1985) *Housing, States and Localities*, Methuen, London; and, for South Wales, K. Morgan and A. Sayer (1988) *Microcircuits of Capital*, Polity, Oxford, chapters 9 and 10.

6. On the 'neighbourhood effect' in British politics see P. Dickens (1988) *One Nation? Social Change and the Politics of Locality*, Pluto, London.

7. K. Marx (1975) 'Critique of Hegel's doctrine of the state', in L. Colletti (ed.) *Marx: Early Writings*, Penguin, Harmondsworth.

8. This point is made in particular by J. Urry (1981) *The Anatomy of Capitalist Societies*, Macmillan, London; and, at an empirical level in P. Dickens (1988) *One Nation?*, Pluto, London.

9. See, for example, CSE State Group (1979) *Struggle over the State: Cuts and Restructuring in Contemporary Britain*, CSE Books, London.

10. London Edinburgh Weekend Return Group (1979) *In and Against The State*, Pluto, London.

11. R. Pahl (1975) *Whose City?* (2nd edn), Penguin, Harmondsworth; (1977) 'Managers, technical experts and the state', in M. Harloe (ed.), *Captive Cities*, Wiley, Chichester.

12. J. Davies (1972) *The Evangelistic Bureaucrat*, Tavistock, London; K. Young and J. Kramer (1978) *Strategy and Conflict in Metropolitan Housing*, Heinemann, London.

13. M. Harloe, J. Issacharoff and R. Minns (1974) *The Organization of Housing*, Heinemann, London.

14. See P. Saunders (1986) *Social Theory and the Urban Question* (2nd edn), Hutchinson, London, pp. 122 *seq.*

15. For an overview of corporatism see chapter 8 of J. Dearlove and P. Saunders (1984) *Introduction to British Politics*, Polity, Oxford.

16. See B. Jessop (1980) 'The transformation of the state in postwar Britain' in R. Scase (ed.) *The State in Western Europe*, Croom Helm, London.

17. M. Foucault (1977) *Discipline and Punish: the Birth of the Prison*, Pantheon, New York; A. Giddens (1985) *The Nation-state and Violence*, Polity, Oxford.

18. A. Giddens (1985) ibid., p. 181.

19. A. Giddens (1985) ibid., p. 193.

20. A. Giddens (1985) ibid., p. 196.

21. A. Giddens (1985) ibid., pp. 196–7.

22. M. Dear and J. Wolch (1987) *Landscapes of Despair*, Polity, Oxford.

23. M. Olson (1965) *The Logic of Collective Action*, Harvard University Press, Cambridge, Mass.

24. J. Goldthorpe, D. Lockwood, F. Bechhoffer and J. Platt (1968) *The Affluent Worker: Political Attitudes and Behaviour*, Cambridge University Press, Cambridge.

25. C. Offe and H. Wisenthal (1980) 'Two logics of collective action: theoretical notes on social class and organisational form', in M. Zeitlin (ed.) *Political Power and Social Theory*, Connecticut University Press, Greenwich, Conn.

26. M. Savage (1987) *The Dynamics of Working-class Politics*, Cambridge University Press, Cambridge, p. 13.

27. 'The uncanny and coercive characteristics of group formations, which are shown in the phenomena of suggestion that accompany them, may therefore with justice be traced back to the origin from the primal horde. The leader of the group is still the dreaded primal father; the group still wishes to be governed by unrestricted force; it has an extreme passion for authority; in Le-Bon's phrase, it has a thirst for obedience'. S. Freud (1985) *Civilization and Its Discontents*, Vol. 12 of Penguin Freud Library, Harmondsworth, p. 160.

28. E. Fromm (1984) *The Working Class in Weimar Germany*, Berg Publishers, Leamington Spa, Warwickshire.

29. W. Reich (1932) *The Mass Psychology of Fascism*, Farrar, Strauss & Giroux, New York.

30. W. Reich (1932) ibid., p. xi.

31. W. Reich (1932) ibid., p. xiii.

32. W. Reich (1932) ibid., p. xv.

33. W. Reich (1932) ibid., p. 63.

34. W. Reich (1932) ibid., p. 38.

35. Quoted in J. Stern (1984) *Hitler: The Fuhrer and the People*, Flamingo, London, p. 18.

36. Quoted in J. Stern (1984) ibid., p. 90.

37. On the persistence of nationalism in contemporary politics see, in particular, A. Smith (1981) *The Ethnic Revival*, Cambridge University Press, Cambridge.

38. P. Van den Berghe (1981) *The Ethnic Phenomenon*, Elsevier, New York.

39. S. Hall's original paper has been published in *The Hard Road to Renewal*, Verso, London, 1988.

40. B. Jessop *et al.* (1984) 'Authoritarian populism, two nations and Thatcherism', *New Left Review*, 147: 32–60.

41. J. Rose (1988) 'Getting away with murder', *New Statesman and Society*, 22 July, p. 35.

42. On the dependency culture which, according to New Right theorists, is a result of extensive state intervention see, for example, M. and R. Friedman (1980) *Free to Choose*, Secker & Warburg, London.

6

LOCALE: THE DESIGN OF SOCIAL RELATIONS?

We now use the themes established in Chapters 1 and 2 to examine the relationships between 'locales' (or spaces designated to certain uses) and individual or social behaviour. The idea that 'locale' affects such behaviour, and can indeed be used to manipulate people's activities, has a long history.[1]

Through 'panopticism' and designating what Giddens would call 'regions' as zones where certain kinds of activity are supposed to take place, and combining such a design with some kind of regulatory regime, it is in principle possible to regulate moral careers and relations between individuals and social groups. Clearly, such a proposal puts architects and town planners in key positions as regards affecting people's lives. By, for example, classifying a space as a prison cell, and making it visible to another space where a prison governor may be observing it, it is theoretically possible to change the prisoner's outlook on life and thereby create beneficial effects for society at large. Thus, careful design (combined with authorities presumed to be working in the general interest) results in modified moral careers and a generally improved social order.

The highpoint of such thinking occurred in the mid to late nineteenth century; a time when, significantly, the architectural profession was establishing itself and attempting to acquire a new area of expertise with which to justify itself.[2] But this kind of thinking received an extra boost with the so-called modern movement in architecture and town planning which became established in the 1920s and 1930s.[3] The architects of the Bauhaus, as well as some of the leading figures of the profession such as Le Corbusier, sincerely believed that, in conjunction with other profes-

(a)

Figure 6.1 Van Dyke Housing Estate, New York. This development followed the precepts of 'modern movement' architectural design. (a) Newman argues that the expansive central grounds are poorly designed for productive use. High-rise buildings are isolated from it and, consequently, serve no effective surveillance function in monitoring activity on the project's grounds. (b) Entrances are 'back' regions which cannot be easily monitored by those receiving visitors. Unfamiliar people can, therefore, enter easily. (From O. Newman, *Defensible Space*, Collier, New York, 1972, p. 43.)

sionals, they were in a position to alter society for the better through the medium of physical design.

Le Corbusier, for example, made extensive proposals for what he called 'the town of tomorrow'. As part of this town he proposed very large scale groups of flats, the purpose of which was to create relatively autonomous communities. Here is description of such a unit:

The idea of grouping 660 flats, which means 3,000 to 4,000 inhabitants, in such a block of closed cell-like elements is to make of them a sort of community, the creation of which would bring about freedom through order. There would be six staircase wells and six entrance halls to serve the 660 flats on the five storeys. . . . The ground floor of these housing blocks would form an immense workshop for household economy: here are the commissariat, the restaurant service, domestic service and laundering.[4]

(b)

Design, including the design of whole towns as well as the design of relatively small-scale living units, therefore became part of a driving social ambition; one which would sweep away the vestiges and miseries of nineteenth century industrial development and create a modern way of life. And for Le Corbusier modernity was primarily equated with a collective and communal way of life.

All these notions found a major realisation in the period following the Second World War. In the British case, the architects' and town planners' ideals were literally concretised in the form of large-scale blocks of flats. Few of them contained the wide range of collective facilities proposed by Le Corbusier (the commissariats, restaurant services and domestic services were conspicuous by their absence) but many were erected by socially conscious, if not necessarily socialist, city authorities.[5]

The question is, of course, were the original ideals recognised? Did better lives and societies result? Or was their effect actually to worsen the living conditions of their inhabitants? There is now a growing argument that designs such as those proposed by the modern movement in architecture and planning, far from creating better societies, are actually the breeding-grounds for a very wide range of social ills. In short, locale is indeed having effects on individuals and societies, but these are of a wholly malevolent and undesirable kind.

The arguments started with Oscar Newman's assertions concerning the relationships between housing design and criminal or anti-social behaviour.[6] On the basis of a survey of a range of New York public housing projects he suggested that schemes with small areas of semi-public space observable by small groups of residents are likely to attract low rates of mugging, robbery and personal assault. This, he suggested, is because residents were able to oversee who was coming to visit them and this in turn warns-off unfamiliar and hostile intruders. Such estates are in effect self-policing. (See Figures 6.1, 6.2.)

These arguments continued with the more recent work of Alice Coleman.[7] She too suggests that high-rise public sector housing generates a very wide range of social problems. We should note here that most of this housing was built during the 1960s, a time when public sector housing was being built on a large scale and owner-occupation stood at around two-fifths of households compared with the current figure of around two-thirds. This in turn meant that public sector housing did not then have the low status and esteem which it now has.

Coleman argued that this housing is now associated with high levels of graffiti, vandalism, litter and excrement. More specifically, she sees the

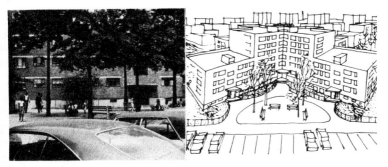

Figure 6.2 Brownsville Housing Estate, New York. Newman argues that 'the building dispositions at Brownsville create triangular buffer areas which are used for play, sitting and parking. These areas are easily observed from the street and from the apartment windows. Entry to buildings is typically from the street through these buffer zones. Residents regard these areas as an extension of their own buildings and maintain active surveillance over them.' Entrances have been turned into 'front' regions. (From O. Newman, *Defensible Space*, Collier, New York, 1972, p. 45.)

design of this accommodation as contributing to such problems. Like Newman, she argues that vandalism and so forth take place in zones where residents are unable to keep a watch over who is entering or leaving their estates. More recently, Coleman has suggested that children brought up in this type of environment are being permanently damaged psychologically.

In short, both Newman and Coleman lend support to the widely held view that high-rise public sector blocks of flats are wholly undesirable places in which to live. Not only are such buildings popularly associated with vandalism and poor quality accommodation but they are also seen as ideal 'back region' breeding grounds for mugging and other forms of violence. Both Newman's and Coleman's suggestions for reform incorporate spatial rearrangements. Coleman suggests, for example, that continuous walkways should be broken up, leaving no possibility of alternative escape-routes. She even implies that a systematic reduction of the buildings' heights would also do much to reduce the array of problems she has found. Finally, she recommends that local authority tenure should give way to other tenure-forms, her preference being owner-occupation or some form of housing association. Newman also suggested that the social problems he observed could be overcome by means of physical planning.

He again recommended that public space for which no residents are accountable should be divided up, smaller semi-public zones being linked to specific groups of tenants. As such, they would be transformed into what Goffman calls 'front regions'.

Coleman's views have become particularly well known, not least because her proposals have recently been adopted with some alacrity by the British government. A number of public sector estates are now receiving what might be called 'the Coleman treatment'. This entails physical modifications such as the removal of alternative means of escape for potential attackers and the transfer of the housing stock to other tenures including owner-occupation. But Coleman's analysis has also become subject to a wide range of criticisms.

First there are the criticisms which challenge Coleman's assertions on their own terms. Hillier and his colleagues argue that the answer to the kinds of problems described by Coleman and Newman is not to create separate, closed off units of definable space which in some sense belong to residents.[8] Rather, they argue, the solution should be to open up the physical infrastructure of the city. Strangers should be encouraged to walk through all parts of the city. They, it is argued, are just as likely to stop a mugging or an act of vandalism as the permanent residents who are under attack. Another reason for a physical opening up of the city is to allow people to get a sense of how their particular part of an urban area relates to the whole. They would be neither socially nor physically separated from the rest of the town. Hillier *et al.* argue that contemporary urban planning has made a number of mistakes in this respect. It is argued that planners, in their attempt to construct small-scale community life through the manipulation of physical spaces, have actually created isolated and dangerous zones. Mediaeval and pre-industrial towns, by contrast, gave to people a better sense of how their district related to the city as a whole.

But a more fundamental critique of Coleman's work is that it is not sufficiently 'social'. Spicker argues, for example, that crime, vandalism and environmental decline have very little to do with the physical environment itself and a great deal to do with public sector tenants' poverty and British local authorities' lack of funds for the maintenance of their housing stock.[9] The same points could be made of Newman. Furthermore, even Hillier *et al.* still seem to be attributing far too much significance to physical space as itself generating certain forms of behaviour. These authors might be well advised to use Giddens's notion of 'locale'. This, as we have seen in Chapter 1, is space socially designated for particular 'front' or 'back' activities rather than space *per se*.

The question is, however, whether academic commentators and critics who give such overwhelming emphasis to social relations and processes are indeed wholly correct to dismiss the kinds of ideas being advanced by Newman, Coleman and Hillier. It may be that these latter analysts do indeed overemphasise the social role of space. They do not give sufficient attention to how spatial relations are mediated by property and other relations and how these lead to residents' feelings of either insecurity or outright fear. But it is also highly probable that widespread popular concerns and perceptions of public sector housing cannot be dismissed as wholly incorrect or the result of false consciousness. Perhaps people actually experiencing contemporary mass public sector housing following the Le Corbusian prototype have detected something which relatively comfortable theoreticians have not. Could it be that the academics, referring solely to political economy and social processes, are actually failing to appreciate some deep-lying aspects of social and individual life? More specifically, could it be that they have systematically ignored the very issues that have been emphasised throughout this analysis: defence of self and kin, territoriality, personal identity and social esteem?

The strong feelings generated by Newman and Coleman suggest that they have. As a result, commonsense or 'lay' theories are nearer the mark than those held by many academics. Furthermore, academic theorists have attempted to explain people's behaviour primarily with reference to the social order and with no reference to the biotic order. The conceptual framework we have been developing would attribute a much more central place to these authors' work. Newman and Coleman have, albeit in a spontaneous and relatively atheoretical way, stumbled into the very aspects of individual and social behaviour which this book proposes have gone missing from contemporary urban sociology. It seems, on reflection, quite likely that certain designs and tenures are associated with certain forms of social and individual behaviour. These authors are allowing for the possibility that territoriality and property are indeed essential to people's sense of well-being or 'ontological security'. Housing developments which do not provide such a sense may well generate all kinds of anti-social behaviour. In short, the required explanations are not wholly social or 'manmade'.

Having admitted that these authors are indeed making some extremely instructive observations, they can also be criticised. Ontological security and territoriality can be found and established in a very diverse set of ways, and, as we have seen throughout this book, they are not simply associated with people's homes, even though housing may be an important part of people's sense of personal security. Furthermore, precisely the same building can encapsulate very different forms of social significance at different stages in its history. A public sector housing estate in Britain or New York in the late twentieth century may well be a threatening place for its tenants and a zone of low social prestige. But this does not necessarily imply that all high-rise public sector housing at all times has these qualities. Indeed, it may well not have been in France at the time that Le Corbusier was advancing his proposals. The work of Newman and Hillier seems particularly associated with the 1970s, 1980s and 1990s, a time when public sector housing is primarily occupied by especially vulnerable social groups, especially those dependent on state support. Meanwhile, public sector tenants have become increasingly marginalised and stigmatised relative to owner-occupiers.

What are the general lessons of these debates on the causal significance of locale on social behaviour? We can begin to make some progress by referring once more to the expressive and biotic orders as discussed in Chapters 1 and 2. We noted there, however, that we should envisage these as closely intertwined with the social and 'cultural' order.

Locales can be seen as front or back regions containing front or back activities. Such regionalisation is, nevertheless, highly contested. On the one hand, owners and designers of buildings are characteristically attempting to determine what should be seen and experienced as front or back regions. On the other hand, the users and observers of buildings and locales are able to experience and interpret physical environments in their own distinct ways.

Such contestations, as we noted in the last chapter, can be seen as the product of relatively straightforward power struggles between opposing individuals and social groups. Fronts and backs are a means through which surveillance and regulation takes place. But there is another, more subtle means through which such struggles occur. This takes the form of architectural discourses analogous to the expressive order of conversation. For distinct localities and societies at distinct times there is a broad consensus (one tending to serve the interests of dominant social groups) as to how physical environments are to be interpreted. Such popular consensus is, nevertheless, notoriously subject to change.[10]

In the 1960s, for example, there was widespread acceptance of the progressive and reassuring 'fronts' projected by high-rise state housing developments. By the 1980s, however, the imagery associated with the same buildings had undergone a dramatic transformation. In Britain, though not in all societies and, indeed, not in all parts of Britain itself, high-rise public sector developments had come to signify social marginalisation and bureaucratic control. So high-rise now broadly signifies 'back region' while other architectural languages (for example 'vernacular' or 'postmodern') signify 'front'.

How are such changes to be explained? On the one hand, changing architectural symbolism clearly reflects broad economic and political change; the rise in owner-occupation, for example, and the decline of state spending on housing. At the same time, it is also a reflection of the processes discussed in Chapters 1 and 2. Identity and security now tend to be sought through individualism and personal effort. Architectural languages partly reflect these changing dominant values; but like these values they are also always open to re-evaluation and change.

NOTES AND REFERENCES

1. For a general survey on the relation between society and space (or locale) see A. King (ed.) (1980) *Buildings and Society*, Routledge & Kegan Paul, London.

2. On architectural determinism in the nineteenth century see, for example, T. Markus (1982) *Order in Space and Society*, Mainstream, Edinburgh.

3. Still the best read on the modern movement in architecture is R. Banham (1960) *Theory and Design in the First Machine Age*, Architectural Press, London.

4. Le Corbusier (1929) *The City of Tomorrow*, Rodker, London.

5. On the adoption of high-rise housing solutions in postwar Britain see, in particular, P. Dunleavy (1981) *The Politics of Mass Housing in Britain, 1945–1975*, Oxford University Press, Oxford.

6. O. Newman (1972) *Defensible Space: Crime Prevention through Urban Design*, Collier, New York.

7. A. Coleman (1985) *Utopia on Trial*, Shipman, London.

8. B. Hillier (1988) 'City of Alice's dreams', *Architects Journal*, 9 July; B. Hillier, J. Hanson, J. Peponis *et al.* (1983) 'Space syntax: a different urban perspective', *Architects Journal*, **30**:11; B. Hillier *et al.* (1986–7) 'The architecture of community', *Architecture and Behaviour*, 3.

9. R. Spicker (1987) 'Poverty and depressed estates: a critique of *Utopia on Trial*', *Housing Studies*, 2 April. See also P. Dickens (1986) 'Review of

Utopia on Trial', *International Journal of Urban and Regional Research*, **10**
297–300.

10. On the problems of architectural communication and symbolism see, for
example, P. Dickens (1981) 'The hut and the machine', *Architectural Design*
51 (1): 32–45. Important in the context of our general analysis is Appleton's
well-known 'prospect-refuge' theory which suggests that people's genetic
makeup leads them to feel attracted to certain kinds of landscape. Drawing
on evolutionary theory and sociobiology, he suggests that people are
instinctively drawn to landscapes which allow them to see without being seen
or to be concealed from enemies. See J. Appleton (1975) *The Experience of
Landscape*, Wiley, Chichester; and J. Appleton (1988) *Environmental
Aesthetics*, Cambridge University Press, Cambridge. He severely under-
estimates, however, the extent to which these instincts are socially mediated.

7

SOCIETY, LOCALITY AND HUMAN NATURE

It has now become one of the great cries amongst geographers and sociologists that people's interpretations of their social and physical surroundings must be incorporated into social theory. Urban sociology has made great strides in understanding the broad structural relations and processes having an impact on people's lives. But there is still lacking an adequate appreciation of how people, actively monitoring their lives and circumstances, are caught up in and influence these circumstances.

We have attempted to rectify these problems. Reinterpreting the Chicago School of Urban Sociology and using the work of contemporary writers such as Goffman, Giddens and Harré has allowed us to make some inroads. Perhaps the main conclusion is that sociology, if it is to systematically address questions of locality and the globalisation, or stretching, of social life, will have to move beyond some of its conceptual and theoretical boundaries, the main aim again being to gain a better understanding of human agency. As we have suggested, a step in this direction is to address the 'new psychology' as represented by Harré *et al.* And it must take more seriously the insights of ethology and sociobiology: work which has still not adequately found its way into social theory.

This catholicity, or openness to alternative perspectives, applies even more to urban sociology. The dominant political economy perspectives which we have reviewed must also be incorporated into work which gives greater emphasis to those mechanisms internal to human beings and which are also deeply influencing their social behaviour. Furthermore, some quite unfashionable functionalist sociology also has much to offer. Nevertheless, we have insisted that there is no question of existing

165

approaches, such as those stemming from Marxism, being abandoned
Rather, they need combining with the less familiar perspectives.

This concluding chapter lays out a conceptual framework which allow
us to start combining an understanding of the instinctive bases o
individual and social behaviour with perspectives emphasising 'manmade
social or cultural relations. Such a framework, one developed on the basi
of a 'realist' approach to explanation, represents a co-ordinating devic
for the range of themes and arguments encountered in earlier chapters.

COMBINING 'THE NATURAL' WITH 'THE SOCIAL'

A first step in constructing a framework which allows us to build a
understanding of people as active beings is to question an assumptio
which seems to have underpinned Western philosophy. Underlying mos
of our earlier analysis is a dualism between, on the one hand, processe
and relationships which are deemed to be 'social' or 'manmade' and thos
which are deemed to be 'natural', 'instinctive' or associated with othe
species besides *homo sapiens*.

This division is characteristic of many of the biological and psycho
logical sciences. It perhaps comes across most clearly with the work of th
early human ethologists and sociobiologists. Some of these writer
(especially those of the 'pop' variety) insist that almost all individual an
social behaviour stems from our genetic inheritance. Even work of th
'non-pop' variety makes similar assumptions about there being mechan
isms, processes and relationships which remain largely untouched b
social or cultural relations. Freud made universal claims of this kind, an
even the less deterministic biologists often leave us unclear as to how thei
work relates to the social and political world.

Meanwhile, social science has also managed to remain almost entirel
immune from the insights (many of them of a dramatic and far-reachin
nature) made by sciences such as evolutionary biology and psychology
Social scientists, and sociologists in particular, may well admit that ther
are innate human instincts, but they will quickly add that these are eithe
relatively unimportant in terms of explaining social behaviour or tha
they are 'socially constructed'. Neither response is satisfactory. Once it i
admitted that there are indeed innate processes affecting behaviour, som
attempt must be made to incorporate them into our understanding. T
say, moreover, that they are 'socially constructed' is only begging th

question. *How* are they socially constructed? *How* are we to understand how such social construction has taken place?

So how are we to proceed? Firstly we must recognise that no one discipline has a monopoly of wisdom. Sociological determinisms such as those represented by certain brands of Marxism are often alienating to such scientific disciplines as psychology and evolutionary biology. Similarly, sociologists have been understandably repelled by the global, ahistorical and sometimes contentious claims of those sciences which do not seem to touch on 'manmade' social or cultural relations. These two groups continue to talk past each other. The dualism is further reinforced.

A way forward is implied by Benton's recent discussion of 'humanism' and 'speciesism' in the early work of Marx.[1] Benton argues that Marx's work suffers from just the kind of dualism we are trying to avoid. Marx maintained, for example, that animals' lives are relatively spontaneous and organised around individual needs while human beings have the capacity to reflect on their actions and to work as groups in a purposeful manner. More importantly for us, Marx and most other social scientists argue that this same dualism applies to human beings. On the one hand, *within* individuals there are animal instincts but, superimposed over these basic instincts are those specifically associated with human beings. This in itself seems fair enough, but it is all too easy to idealise these latter instincts as wholly 'good' and beneficial to the human and natural worlds.

Benton argues that this dualism should be questioned, especially in the light of growing contemporary concerns with people's relationships to other species. This new approach entails recognising that to some extent all living beings are 'natural beings'. They all have natural needs and instincts (such as nutrition and sexual reproduction) and all have powers and capacities enabling them to satisfy these needs. Each species, nevertheless, has distinct ways of interacting with nature, these interactions confirming its 'species life' or characteristic mode of existence. So, although all organisms are natural beings, the precise way in which each species survives and reproduces (through, for example, nutrition, shelter and biological reproduction) varies according to the species in question. This, of course, means that the range of ways in which species' needs are met is, in Benton's words, 'almost unimaginably diverse'.

Such is a starting-point for our approach. It implies that when we come to human organisms we should not be concerned as a matter of principle with separating 'human' from 'animal' needs but with examining the specifically *human* ways in which people do what other animals do. Human beings have, of course, distinct ways of, for example, satisfying their needs for food or biological reproduction. They have a need in common with other animals for feelings of security, but again the precise ways in which these are, or indeed are not, achieved, are distinctly human. This approach can even be extended to those areas of human life which are deemed to be wholly 'human'. Aesthetics, cognition and self-realisation are almost certainly specifically *human* concerns, but they nevertheless have some basis in the needs which are common to all species.

So the general approach here is one recognising a relatively high degree of communality between human beings with other living organisms while at the same time recognising the special and distinctive qualities of human beings; especially those of conceptualisation and language. Human beings (who often, though by no means always, have progressed beyond the sphere of needing to satisfy basic needs such as hunger) have established ways of meeting their species needs which they as a conceptualising species find socially, politically or even aesthetically satisfying. Such are Benton's propositions. There remain, however, substantial difficulties when it comes to putting them into practice. We now address these difficulties.

SOCIETY, SPACE AND INSTINCTS: DEVELOPING A REALIST ANALYSIS

The foregoing arguments have significant implications for how we draw together the various themes discussed in earlier chapters. More specifically, they suggest how to deal with the dualism between the 'social' on the one hand and the 'natural' on the other. We must now explore how we might start constructing a more unified approach, one in which we envisage the innate biological and psychic drives underlying people's lives (what the Chicago School would have called the biotic order) as mediated by social and cultural processes and relations. At the same time, we must recognise that some of these social or cultural relations and processes are themselves partly a product of human beings' innate demands as a species. In other words, culture and society are not simply manmade by conscious human beings. They are also a product of the biotic order.

The first key point to emphasise is our insistence on the communality between human beings and other organisms. Secondly, and equally important, is our insistence that the various ways in which people meet their basic needs (and indeed go well beyond meeting them) are constructed by the society in which they live. This means that we envisage social change in terms of there being certain underlying mechanisms and processes which human beings share with all living organisms. It also means that we envisage the precise ways in which these processes take place as mediated by the cultural and social world. Furthermore, it is now the case that *homo sapiens*, in all 'his' wisdom, has found ways of not only destroying other species but of obliterating himself. This means that there is, in fact, no reason why the 'necessary' mechanisms underlying human and animal survival are inevitable or indeed necessary at all. Such is the growing recognition of the contemporary environmental movement.

This reference to 'necessary' mechanisms and the contingent circumstances in which they operate implies a realist approach to integrating the natural with the social sciences. It is this approach which, in a more developed form, offers the most satisfactory means of combining the various forms of understanding discussed earlier.

Realism as an explanatory framework in the social sciences has been widely discussed elsewhere.[2] It is now finding extended use in urban and regional sociology, largely as a reaction to the positivism and empiricism associated with the earliest forms of geographical analysis. Realism was originally advanced, however, in opposition to idealism, the notion put forward by Berkeley and others that there is no reality other than that which can be perceived. It is, therefore, argued by idealists that reality is a mental construct: human understanding being limited to direct experience of external objects. Realism makes, however, what seems like a commonsensical assumption that there is indeed a reality which exists even if it does not have what Berkeley called 'sensible qualities'. In other words, a thing does not need to be perceived as 'real' for it actually to exist.

A realist approach to explanation makes a crucial distinction between the abstract and the concrete. Figure 7.1 should be referred to as a means of conceptualising this perspective. Abstract theory and research tend to focus on general relations, structures and causal mechanisms at the upper levels of Figure 7.1. It is here that the most substantial theoretical claims are made. However, these relations and mechanisms are seen only as latent or potential. Their precise observed forms, indeed whether their latent powers are released for observation at all, depend on contingent circumstances. An illustration that is sometimes given here is that of gunpowder. It has the latent capacity to explode, but whether it actually does so depends on 'contingent' circumstances. Is it damp? Is it connected

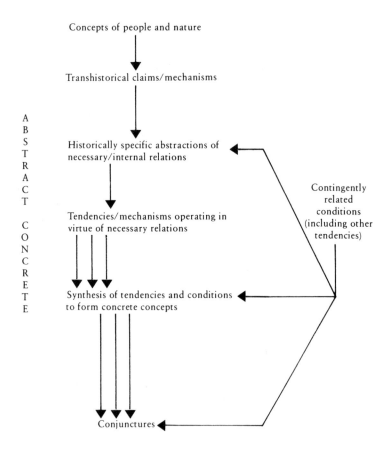

Figure 7.1 A realist approach to explanation. (After Dickens *et al.* 1985.)

to an exploding device? Does someone actually press a button? Clearly, an explanation of an explosion requires an understanding both of the latent powers of gunpowder as well as an appreciation of the contingent circumstances of the explosion.

So a realist approach to causality first focuses on latent properties. Explanation is achieved through identifying how these properties behave under the conditions to which they are subject. The prime task of theory is that of identifying causal mechanisms and tendencies. The crucial distinction is made between these relations and tendencies and those which are seen as contingent. The latter has less explanatory weight but, very importantly, they are not seen as in any sense secondary. They determine not only when and how the gunpowder goes off, they may even be deeply implicated in whether the gunpowder goes off at all.

How this kind of framework is applied to social analysis varies considerably. In contemporary urban and regional sociology it has been almost exclusively allied to Marxism.[3] Abstract theory, for example, interprets 'underlying' and 'necessary' relations as those between capital and wage labour. The tendencies operating in virtue of these relations include, for example, the concentration of capital, deskilling, the steady displacement of living labour by capital and the law of value dictating prices at which commodities can be profitably sold on the world market. Meanwhile, 'contingent circumstances' include, for example, those appertaining to a particular locality at a particular time. How, even whether, capitalist enterprises are developing and operating depends on the particular conjuncture of class and other kinds of social relations in the society or epoch in question. Local outcomes or 'conjunctures' may, on rare occasions, be the result of the actions of people in the particular locality. More typically, however, they are the result of underlying latent tendencies within capitalism as a whole, combined with the particularities of the locality, region or nation.

Other theoreticians with different preoccupations would ascribe the category of 'necessary/internal relations' in quite different ways. For example, Harré suggests that there are deep-rooted, innate causal mechanisms influencing individual and social behaviour. The mechanisms involved are largely based on theories derived from psychology. As we have seen, Harré and his colleagues suggest that:

[The] ultimate problem for a human being is to make his actions intelligible to others and his situation as he interprets it intelligible to himself, so as to preserve his sense of personal worth.[4]

With such an understanding, a picture of the individual in society can be built on the basis of a general theory of the motives and mechanisms underlying human behaviour. Nevertheless, the particularities of how and whether this happens depends on detailed observations and conversations. The senior white collar workers encountered in Chapter 1, as well as so-called football hooligans and inmates of asylums, all have specific ways of attempting to preserve their self-esteem and sense of personal worth.

What are the problems with realism? One set of difficulties is spelt out by Saunders in his recent discussion of how this epistemology has been applied to urban and regional analysis.[6] His concern is that the theories concerning the underlying mechanisms cannot be adequately tested or falsified. They are insulated from refutation. The assumption is made that there are indeed underlying generating mechanisms, but there can be no real check that the abstract theory is correct about what these mechanisms are. It therefore fails the test of a good theory: it cannot be either repudiated or tested.

More specifically still, Saunders is especially concerned with what he sees as the hijacking of realism by Marxism. Marxist urban sociology, he argues, has undergone great traumas in separating itself from structuralism. But no sooner has it detached itself from the dogmatism and imperialism of structuralist Marxism (of the kind discussed in Chapter 4 in relation to Castells's early work) than it has re-adopted the same dogmas in a more subtle form. The subtlety being more sensitive to local variation and human agency, it nevertheless still assumes that *the* most important underlying causal mechanism is class struggle.

Saunders endorses Hirst's assertion that no epistemology should be awarded the privilege of being applicable outside its own discourse.[7] Hirst argues that 'epistemological principles that lay down the means of developing scientific knowledge cannot exist outside the theories that adopt and apply them'.[8] Saunders's own research strategy adopts an 'ideal type' analysis; a strategy originally developed by Weber. Ideal types ('the city' being a good example) are used in everyday discourse. They are ways in which we all attempt to give some kind of order to a social world which is infinitely complex. But the order which we create out of chaos is clearly one based on our own knowledge and values. Ideal types are used in the construction of working hypotheses: guesses which can be evaluated, confirmed or rejected by testing against empirical evidence.

Saunders's points are well taken. His main contribution is to recognise that what are some people's 'necessary' relations and processes are other people's 'contingent' ones. To take two examples drawn from earlier parts of this book, a Marxist's 'necessary' capital–labour relations are, to a sociobiologist, mere contingencies. But to a Marxist or someone working within a political economy framework, the insights of evolutionary biology or contemporary psychology are usually attributed insignificant explanatory weight. Again, each discipline finishes by talking past the other. 'Theoretical terrorism' again ensues, with each discipline asserting that *it* is the one with the *real* explanation. We will shortly discuss ways of dealing with this problem.

Saunders's proposals still leave substantial difficulties. Firstly, it is actually very difficult to extend the methods of the natural sciences to an understanding of the social world. Hypotheses about the social world cannot be 'proved' or 'disproved' simply by examining empirical evidence as though it were taking place within a sealed test tube. The social sciences are usually dealing with what Sayer calls 'open systems'. Relationships within the particular objects or processes under study are not necessarily constant. More important still, the relationships between these objects and processes and the external conditions under which they are operating are also subject to constant change. This means that we may well find regularities and similarities between different systems but it is virtually impossible to assume from such similarities that the same causes and mechanisms are at work. Observing 'regularity' cannot be assumed to derive from similar causes. One approach (and this seems to lie behind ideal type analysis) is simply to treat the system under study *as if* it were closed; effectively ignoring the remainder of the social world. But this ostrich-like behaviour is surely unsatisfactory. It is not a realistic way of avoiding the difficulty of hypothesis testing and refutation in the social sciences.

Secondly, and quite apart from the difficulty of hypothesis testing, there is a problem concerning ideal types themselves. These, it will be remembered, are not hypotheses but means for the construction of hypotheses. Ideal types are therefore mental constructs, the result of someone's experience, interests and values. But it is difficult to know what status to attach to them. If a hypothesis is abandoned does this place a question mark over the ideal type? Or does the ideal type remain good however many hypotheses are tested and refuted? Furthermore, do we simply assume that one person's ideal type is as good as the next person's? As Sayer argues:

[Ideal type methodology] pays no attention to the structure of the world and hence is unable to recognise that some selections are better than others according to their relationship to this structure.[9]

In the end it is very difficult to see how ideal type analysis evades the charge of empiricism. On the other hand, Saunders and others are surely right to comment adversely on how realism has been applied to the social sciences. If 'necessary internal relations' remains interpreted as only the class relations to which Marxists give such credence, then this is precisely the kind of interpretation which gives realism a bad name. Quite apart from other kinds of deep-rooted social mechanisms and relations (such as those of gender and race) which some would argue are even more

'necessary' and 'internal' than those of class, there are also innate
relations and processes which are also the behaviour of individuals and
societies.

A way forward is to re-use realism in a way that tries to encompass all
the processes affecting human behaviour and not just the class mechan
isms to which urban sociologists have so far applied a realist framework.
We again recognise that individual and social behaviours are generated by
mechanisms and processes which are not necessarily observable. We must
also recognise the extremely important insights and concepts now
emerging from evolutionary biology and social psychology. All are
attempting to gain insights at a fairly abstract level into underlying
processes. These theories get into trouble, however, when first they start
over-extending their abstractions down to the 'concrete' levels of Figure
7.1; and second when they fail to recognise the effects of contingencies;
and third when they deny the relationships *between* the discourses. An
example is early sociobiology.

A sensible escape out of these wholly unnecessary impasses returns us to
some of our earlier propositions regarding the combining of the natural
with the social sciences. The object must be that of constructing some
kind of common discourse encompassing both of these often warring
discourses.

Figure 7.2 represents a first step. It is as much a research agenda as a
fixed statement of absolute truths. It suggests a recognition by all
discourses that at the highest levels of abstraction (those entitled
'concepts of people and nature' and 'transhistorical claims') there are
indeed relations and mechanisms which are common to both human and
non-human organisms. These are 'underlying' and 'necessary' not only for
conceptual clarification but in terms of the reproduction of human life
itself. At the same time, however, it should be noted that the upper level
of Figure 7.2 also recognise that a characteristic feature of human beings
is their capacity to conceptualise themselves and their societies and to
relate themselves to others through the medium of language. Further
more, they can of course reflect on their instincts and the biotic order.
And they can act on such reflection. In brief, Figure 7.2 implies
recognition that human beings are self-aware and self-monitoring in ways
in which other species are not. Indeed, people have used their self
awareness as a means of achieving mastery over other species.

It is at these higher levels of abstraction that evolutionary biology and
ethology can make their strongest claims. People working in these fields

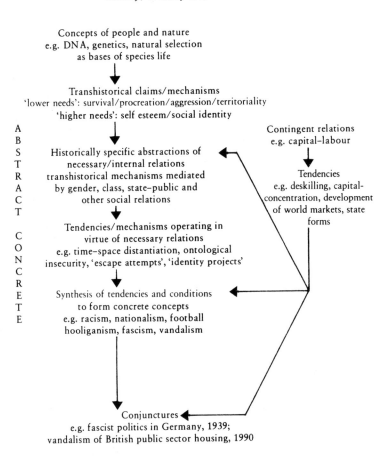

Figure 7.2 Society, locality and human nature: a realist perspective.

would argue (albeit with strong disagreements) that humans share with animals a range of latent forms of behaviour which are genetically inherited. These include sexual reproduction, self-preservation, male aggression (especially by juveniles), kin altruism, the acquisition of property and territorial instincts. Needless to say, these cannot be cleanly separated from each other. Territoriality and aggressive instincts are closely related and these in turn revolve around reproduction, self-preservation and altruism towards kin.

It will be noted that these basic instincts are labelled here 'lower' and 'higher'. Such descriptions follow Maslow and Malinowski.[10] In rather different ways both these authors suggested that human cultures are to a large degree founded upon the instinctive (what Maslow called 'instinctoid') needs of human beings. Most basically, these needs include biological processes, aggressive tendencies and the priority of surviving and procreating. Beyond such drives, Maslow, in particular, recognised that there is for humans a large and complex range of what he called 'higher needs'. These include self-esteem, the respect of others, personal identity and the need to belong to some wider collective groups.

These 'higher needs' are also instinctive. But the point is again that they are realised (or indeed they fail to be realised) through specifically social or 'cultural' means. At this stage the analysis starts to move down Figure 7.2 and to the right, showing 'social' or 'cultural' relations combining with Maslow's 'instinctoid' needs. So again, social institutions and relations are not simply the product of social formations associated with capitalism or any other mode of production. Social relations represent the structures and resources which can both realise and inhibit human beings' needs and demands.

It is often argued by contemporary critical theorists, for example, that the nuclear family and its associated rituals of courtship and marriage are products of capitalism or means of reproducing patriarchal gender relations in the home. The family, and the rituals and institutions with which it is associated, may or may not be serving these functions but it *is* serving the very necessary processes of reproducing and raising the human species. The fact that a version of the family has persisted for so long implies that an explanation may lie as much in the spheres of biology and emotions as in the reproduction of labour power or the oppression of women. Clearly, both processes have become inextricably combined.

Proceeding down Figure 7.2 to 'historically specific abstractions of necessary/internal relations' we find there a range of social relations. These, as the diagram is suggesting, are partly a realisation of the 'necessary' relations and processes stemming from the biotic order of psychological and biological drives. But partly, too, they are a result of the 'contingent' relations and processes to the right of the diagram.

As regards the former types of social relation (those functioning to reproduce the biotic order) our framework here takes its cue from Davis and Moore's functionalist sociology.[11] As long ago as the mid-1940s these authors argued that social stratification can be seen as a necessary function of any relatively complex society. A tendency within any society, with its prerequisite for biological and cultural survival, will be a need for some kind of co-ordinating and controlling social roles. Such positions are functionally necessary for any society to service and reproduce itself.

Davis and Moore argued, however, that such controlling positions are not necessarily easy to fill. They require long training and there may be a shortage of willing personnel. Key jobs for the functioning and reproduction of society must bring with them special privileges and rewards. So, for Davis and Moore, the fact that virtually all societies have been stratified is a direct product of their need to survive and reproduce themselves.

Needless to say, such views do not secure the immediate approval of much contemporary critical social science. For example, the knee-jerk response from most Marxists to the kind of functionalist sociology represented by Davis and Moore is that they are simply acting as apologists for the status quo, explaining as 'natural' or 'necessary' what is in fact socially derived. Nevertheless, we are insisting here on the possibility that functionalist explanations of this kind may well contain a kernel of truth, even if they do not adequately recognise the extent to which social inequalities and stratifications are also actively made and reproduced by people whose main objectives are self-aggrandisement. Again, Davis and Moore are suggesting that human beings find distinctly 'human' ways of reproducing themselves and their societies, in the way suggested by Benton.

Meanwhile, the social relations and tendencies to the right of Figure 7.2 are labelled here as 'contingent'. They incorporate well-known features of contemporary capitalism. These include not only the relations between capital and wage labour but also deskilling, the concentration of capital, and the gradual opening up of a capitalist world market. Furthermore, 'contingent' is how we have earlier denoted the 'state form' characteristic of contemporary democratic governments. Towards the lower part of Figure 7.2 these contingent relations are combining with tendencies derived from the left-hand side of the diagram (associated with the biotic order) to a 'synthesis of tendencies'. These include many of the processes we have noted earlier: time–space distantiation, ontological insecurity, identity projects and escape attempts. The lowest level of 'conjunctures' are the processes experienced in the real or 'concrete' world. At this level a myriad of social relations and processes are combined with the instinctive forms of behaviour which have evolved within human beings over millions of years. There are a number of closely related lessons to be learned from Figure 7.2. Maslow's 'higher' and 'lower' needs towards the top of the diagram are always socially or culturally mediated and constructed. At the same time, individual and social behaviour, and the institutions associated with this behaviour, represent the specifically human ways in which biological and psychic life are reproduced by human populations. Thus, what the Chicago School called the 'biotic' and 'cultural' orders are closely intertwined.

Finally, and referring back to Figure 2.1 (p.38), we must remind ourselves of the expressive order of people's own understandings and articulations and its links to the biotic and cultural orders. The expressive order reflects not only the social order but the biotic order, this latter including attempts to gain respect, esteem and security. For all the complexities of the expressive order it does, therefore, have common underlying themes: social relations, primordial instincts and people's attempts to manage their moral careers.

In trying to understand the complex and concrete world of 'conjunctures' at the foot of Figure 7.2, commonly used categories such as 'aggression' or 'territoriality' are simultaneously helpful and misleading. They are helpful in so far as they seem to be referring to latent instincts and drives. These, we are suggesting, must indeed form an important part of our understanding of individual and social behaviour. On the other hand, such words do not recognise how such instincts are socially formed or how ideas such as 'aggression' are themselves socially defined. This ambiguity is, therefore, a major problem if we intend using the expressive order itself as an explanation of social relations or social change. On their own, the simplifications used in everyday conversation are still some way from offering adequate understandings. 'Territoriality' or 'aggression' may allude to innate drives, but they cannot explain such diverse behaviours as 'football hooliganism', domestic violence or an inner city uprising. Such concrete events must be combinations of inbred attributes and 'manmade' social relations.[12]

So despite (indeed because of) the fact that words such as 'aggression' are used very widely, an adequate understanding of what is occurring again entails our return to the underlying mechanisms and tendencies affecting people's behaviour. Some of these, such as genetic reproduction or kin altruism are shared with other species. Others (such as the preservation of honour, status and self) are specifically associated with human beings. Both, however, combine with the particular kind of society of which they are part.

NOTES AND REFERENCES

1. T. Benton (1988) 'Humanism = speciesism? Marx on humans and animals', *Radical Philosophy*, **50**: 4–18.

2. My account of realism is largely based on A. Sayer (1984) *Method Social Science*, Hutchinson, London. See also R. Bhaskar (1979) *The Possibility of Naturalism*, Harvester Wheatsheaf, Hemel Hempstead.

3. For an example of the application of realism to Marxist urban theory see, for example, P. Dickens, S. Duncan, M. Goodwin and F. Gray (1985) *Housing, States and Localities*, Methuen, London.

4. R. Harré (1979) *Social Being*, Blackwell, Oxford, pp. 142–3.

5. A. Sayer (1981) 'Abstraction: a realist interpretation', *Radical Philosophy*, **28**: 6–15.

6. See in particular P. Saunders (1986) *Social Theory and the Urban Question*, Hutchinson, London. Especially chapter 6 and the appendix entitled 'A note on the empirical testing of theories'.

7. P. Hirst (1979) *On Law and Ideology*, Macmillan, London, p. 20. Quoted in Saunders (1986) op. cit.

8. Hirst is quoted in P. Saunders (1986) op. cit., p. 354.

9. A. Sayer (1984) op. cit., p. 216.

10. B. Malinowski (1944) *A Scientific Theory of Culture*, Chapel Hill, N. Carolina: A. Maslow (1954) *Motivation and Personality*, Harper & Row, New York.

11. K. Davis and W. Moore (1949) 'Some principles of stratification', *American Sociological Review* (April): 242–47.

12. On the problems surrounding the definition of 'human aggression' see in particular J. Archer and K. Browne (1989) 'Concepts and approaches to the study of aggression', in J. Archer and K. Browne (eds), *Human Aggression*, Routledge, London.

EPILOGUE

This book, on several occasions, criticises contemporary Marxists. Marx himself, however, saw the great intellectual challenge of the nineteenth century as combining the social with the natural sciences.

History is a real part of natural history – of nature developing into man. Natural science will in time incorporate into itself the science of man, just as the science of man will incorporate into itself natural science: there will be one science.[1]

He argued that such a single science would prove liberating for human beings. They would see their place in nature and be educated by it rather than exploit it. Yet, despite such advances as genetics, evolutionary biology and psychology, as well as the many advances in social theory which have been made since his day, Marx's 'one science' has still not been constructed. Indeed, the dichotomy between the natural and the social sciences has, if anything, increased. As this book suggests, a sociology which properly reflects the concerns of the people that it is studying needs to attempt such an integration: exploring how people's instincts combine with the social world and how, at the same time, the social world adapts to people's instinctive behaviour. The exciting possibility remains that urban sociology, with its distinctive focus on how social systems and people combine in locales and localities, could be the discipline from which Marx's 'one science' emerges. A central theme guiding this study (the increasing globalisation of concentration of social systems) makes the construction of this one science an ever more urgent task.

NOTES AND REFERENCES

1. K. Marx (1975) *Early Writings*, Pelican, Harmondsworth, p. 355.

INDEX